Academic Departments

How They Work, How They Change

*Barbara E. Walvoord,
Anna K. Carey, Hoke L.
Smith, Suzanne W. Soled,
Philip K. Way, Debbie Zorn*

*ASHE-ERIC Higher Education Report Volume 27, Number 8
Adrianna J. Kezar, Series Editor*

Prepared and published by

JOSSEY-BASS
A Wiley Company
San Francisco

In cooperation with

ERIC*HE*

*ERIC Clearinghouse on Higher Educa
The George Washington University*
URL: www.eriche.org

T0204645

ASHE

*Association for the Study
of Higher Education*
URL: www.tiger.coe.missouri.edu/~ashe

The
George
Washington
University
WASHINGTON DC

*Graduate School of Education and Human Development
The George Washington University*
URL: www.gwu.edu

Academic Departments: How They Work, How They Change

Barbara E. Walvoord, Anna K. Carey, Hoke L. Smith, Suzanne W. Soled, Philip K. Way, Debbie Zorn

ASHE-ERIC Higher Education Report Volume 27, Number 8
Adrianna J. Kezar, Series Editor

This publication was prepared partially with funding from the Office of Educational Research and Improvement, U.S. Department of Education, under contract no. ED-99-00-0036. The opinions expressed in this report do not necessarily reflect the positions or policies of OERI or the Department.

ISSN 0884-0040   ISBN 0-7879-5714-3

The ASHE-ERIC Higher Education Report is part of the Jossey-Bass Higher and Adult Education Series and is published eight times a year by Jossey-Bass, 350 Sansome Street, San Francisco, California 94104-1342.

For subscription information, see the Back Issue/ Subscription Order Form in the back of this journal.

Prospective authors are strongly encouraged to contact Adrianna Kezar, Director, ERIC Clearinghouse on Higher Education, at (202) 296-2597 ext. 14 or akezar@eric-he-edu.

Visit the Jossey-Bass Web site at www.josseybass.com.

Printed in the United States of America on acid-free recycled paper containing 100 percent recovered waste paper, of which at least 20 percent is postconsumer waste.

EXECUTIVE SUMMARY

Should Departments Change?

In the current environment of economic, political, ideological, and technological pressures on higher education, departments must attend carefully to stakeholders' demands to (a) improve undergraduate student learning, especially in general education; (b) collaborate across disciplines; (c) apply knowledge to community and workplace needs; (d) be more cost-efficient or "productive"; and (e) provide education by alternative means, using technology to transcend boundaries of time and space (Kennedy, 1997, p. 277; Layzell, 1999). But departments must not only respond to the latest societal pressures but also, in a free society, defend values, question societal norms, and freely pursue knowledge. In fulfilling their complex missions, departments must focus not only on what to *do* but also on what to *be*. Though not all departments need to change in the same ways, departments across the nation must reinvent new forms of collegiality and become more outward-oriented, more focused on results, and more entrepreneurial. They must develop new systems to reward their members, enhance productivity, and assure the quality of their work.

How Can Departments Change?

The foundation for departmental reform is Zemsky's concept that "the way to reform is not to circumvent the departmental structure that is endemic to most academic institutions but to enlist that structure in the reform itself" (1991, p. 5A). Those who would change the department must deeply understand it. From that understanding emerge strategies for change. Characteristics of departments emerge from the national literature; each practitioner must use them as a heuristic to question the cultures and structures of his or her own department.

The appendix summarizes the specific traits of departments we discuss and the avenues for change suggested by those traits. Unlike normal businesses, which organize subunits of people around functions aligned for administrative convenience, academic departments organize people of similar disciplinary interests to serve multiple constituencies in ways that allow both innovation and predictability. At its best, the department is the flexible belt, not the fixed cog, that channels intellectual energy into administrative work.

In the department, the core academic values—among them academic freedom, autonomy, collegiality, specialization, and reason—are strong but often in conflict and under attack; change strategies must build upon and redefine these values. The department within its institution is uniquely autonomous yet uniquely interdependent. Change must build on departmental autonomy, but it also requires complex roles from central administrators—provision of shared mission, rich information, fiscal incentives, management of crises and deadlines, support for chairs, alternative structures that enhance or replace traditional departmental tasks, and university governance systems that encourage interdisciplinary collaboration for the common good. If the role of departments is to channel intellectual energy to serve multiple constituencies, then the role of the administration is not to fight the department or master it, but to help it do its proper work.

Departments' internal organization combines elements of the collegium and the bureaucracy as well as oligarchic, political, feudal, and caste-based systems. The collegial model, in which a closely knit group of peers under a consultative leader share work and decision making in collaborative ways, is treasured as an ideal by faculty. Some literature suggests the collegial model is the most successful form of governance in higher education. But traditional collegial forms are stressed as departments take on new roles and new types of non-tenure-track faculty or support staff, and as they conduct education in geographically dispersed or virtual spaces, collaborating in new ways with businesses and with alternative providers. Much of departmental leadership, work, roles, and rewards can be understood as a mixed, transitional response to these new challenges.

Departmental leaders, largely untrained for administration, are torn among multiple allegiances and multiple tasks, and they wield ambiguous power. They must somehow balance bureaucratic work with strategic and visionary functions in order to lead change. Departmental work is determined by multiple influences and by the considerable autonomy of faculty to allocate their time. As increasing numbers of non-tenure-track or geographically dispersed faculty fall outside the traditional modes of collegial interaction and shared norms, departments may lose control of quality, or they may implement more bureaucratic modes of control, such as job distinction by rank and title; assessment of outcomes; and extrinsic rewards. Change must build upon the best of departmental experiments with new modes of ensuring quality.

Departments have traditionally enhanced productivity by hiring new (sometimes low-cost) teaching staff, by increasing class size, and by using technology for research and writing. Still largely wedded to the traditional classroom lecture and testing paradigms, faculty are faced with new paradigms of learning, new demands for education that transcends boundaries of time and space, students with new expectations, and the need for new forms of productivity—which have given rise to pedagogical movements and experiments that are still largely outside the traditional departmental systems of work and rewards. Change must build upon best practice as departments struggle toward new modes.

In short, the department still exhibits the collegial modes and academic values of its original form as a guild of scholars who banded together to sell their services. But it is exhibiting on all fronts the mixed, transitional, and experimental modes that mark its transition to a much more complex world in which it must not only keep up with rapidly changing disciplinary knowledge but also offer increasingly diversified services to an increasingly complex world. Academic departments are not dinosaurs but evolving organisms that are experimenting with new forms and that need help and support to realize the potential for change that their structures imply.

What Types of Strategies Can Departments Use for Change?

Change strategies in the literature fall into six categories: (a) change the environment; (b) change the type of person in the department; (c) address values by building on them, changing them, or resolving conflicts among them; (d) change or build upon the way the department is structured in terms of its organization, its leadership positions, its reward systems, its dispersion of power, or its forums for conversation and decision making; (e) affect the decision-making process in which the department is engaged; or (f) create alternative structures such as institutes or offices of first-year studies to take over some of the department's functions. Because departments differ, strategies from these various categories must be shaped to the department's own characteristics. They must be combined and integrated; no strategy by itself is likely to be sufficient.

What Should Departments Be?

The most important goal is to change not only what a department *does* but also what it *becomes*. The visionary strand of the literature suggests that departments need "collegial entrepreneurialism" or "authentic collegiality" enhanced with "quality" principles. It suggests that departments try to become "learning" departments or "teams." The primary features of the new visions are (a) a department's capacity for self-knowledge, including understanding its culture, environments, assumptions, values, and mental models; (b) systems thinking, which views all elements of an organization as interacting parts; (c) open and productive interaction that encourages closeness, collaboration, minimal defensiveness, and the ability to handle conflict; (d) high freedom for individuals combined with encouragement for individuals to commit to the good of the department; (e) outward focus on interpreting the environment, meeting the needs of stakeholders, and producing results; (f) emphasis on learning from experience; and (g) support for leaders who are collaborative yet who also initiate change and guide the group.

A nationwide initiative to assist departments might offer consulting to departments and institutions, helping them to initiate change and become more effective. The national initiative would also disseminate models of best practice, train department leaders, and conduct research on departmental work and departmental change.

CONTENTS

FOREWORD

Higher education is in the throes of unprecedented change—interdisciplinary research and teaching, assessment, tenure, performance indicators, cost control, diversified student body and faculty, internationalization, environmentalism, technology, and the list goes on. Several critics suggest that one of the barriers to these many changes is the departmental structure. Departments grew in significance over the last century as faculty specialized more narrowly in particular areas of research. They reflect specialized research and teaching fields. Can you imagine universities without academic departments? If you are an administrator or faculty member, probably not. But to anyone else, this structure is often elusive and its importance not apparent.

Critics over the last 30 years have called for the radical dismantling of academic departments. In particular, critics in the 1970s cited departmental structures as a barrier to interdisciplinary teaching and research and to the application of research to real-world problems that were not encapsulated in any one discipline. This last decade has seen numerous concerns about the continued viability of the structure of academic departments. Yet Barbara Walvoord and her coauthors recommend a very different direction from that of previous commentators. They suggest that enlisting the academic departmental structure rather than trying to circumvent it can fulfill the changes the public and the politicians desire. The authors' main premise is that the department can be used as a lever to create change if people who instigate change understand the culture of departments. Walvoord and her coauthors spent several years engaged in an intensive study of change in eight departments and in programs that enlisted many other departments in change efforts. Their careful research can be a guide for campuses across the country.

Understanding the departmental culture means examining the academic values that have been associated with this structure, such as collegiality, autonomy, academic freedom, and specialization. By understanding these values, change agents can build on them, redefine them, or work to change them if they appear to conflict with the direction of change. But, the authors argue, the first step is to understand the structure, in order to make the needed and appropriate structural modifications.

Understanding the close connection between the department and the discipline is another important lever. Institutional change can be accomplished through the disciplinary societies. Several national efforts already are attempting to facilitate change through the disciplines. For example, the American Association for Higher Education has used the disciplines as a base for integrating service-learning into the curriculum. The Council for Graduate Schools and the Association for American Colleges and Universities manage a project called Preparing Future Faculty that works with the disciplinary societies to educate graduate students as to their future roles as professors, which, it is hoped, will affect the culture of departments.

Walvoord and her coauthors also place the work on departments within the broader university, illustrating how centralized resources and administrative units, unions, students, and others can affect departmental power. All the different external forces and conditions can be used in equalizing power or creating change. This monograph also suggests the importance of departmental leadership (vis-à-vis the department chair) and the need for administrators to foster the commitment and ability of this crucial change agent. The authors have two suggested strategies for fostering greater understanding of departmental culture—a national information center and the development of learning departments. The learning department is one that has conducted self-analysis, understands the values, disciplinary connection, power, socialization, reward system, and leadership, and uses this information to operate more effectively.

The authors caution that understanding departmental culture is only one aspect of many strategies necessary to create change on college campuses. Other ASHE-ERIC monographs that might assist your campus in engaging the change process include *The Leadership Compass* by Wilcox and Ebbs, *Benchmarking in Higher Education* by Alstete, *Quality: Transforming Postsecondary Education* by Chaffee and Sherr, *Redesigning Higher Education* by Gardiner, and *Renewing the College and Departmental Curriculum* by Toombs and Tierney. Each of these monographs provides insight into other important change strategies, among them leadership, management tools, the quality paradigm, campus dialogues, and faculty development. This volume is very different from other resources on change in higher education, a growing area of research. It highlights a key ingredient missing in most change studies: understanding the core institutional structure within higher education.

Adrianna Kezar
Series Editor

ACKNOWLEDGMENTS

We owe a great debt to former members of our team who contributed to the research and thinking that informed this volume: James McDonough, who served as a codirector of the University of Cincinnati's Project to Improve and Reward Teaching (PIRT) and as associate dean of the College of Engineering, and who is currently dean of Clermont College of the University of Cincinnati; and Kristen Pool, who, when she worked with our research team, was a graduate student in English and an intern for the Writing Across the Curriculum program at the University of Cincinnati.

We are also grateful to the 58 PIRT departments at the University of Cincinnati for the rich ideas and the spirit of collegiality they brought to PIRT. We especially thank the faculty and chairs from the eight PIRT departments we studied in detail; they contributed hours of their time for interviews with us, shared their documents with us, and invited us to their departmental meetings. We appreciate also the support and encouragement that PIRT has received from the University of Cincinnati central administration and deans, especially Provost Anthony Perzigian. We thank Adrianna Kezar, our editor at ASHE-ERIC, for her faith in our manuscript and her patience as the book slowly took shape. Our thanks also go to Daniel Wheeler, who offered helpful comments on an earlier version of the manuscript, and to the anonymous reviewers. Cecilia Lucero contributed to the content of "Departmental Work, Faculty Roles, and Rewards," and she and Gwen Hagey-Shirk made an invaluable contribution to the final checking and assembling of the manuscript.

INTRODUCTION

The way to reform is not to circumvent the departmental structure that is endemic to most academic institutions but to enlist that structure in the reform itself.
(Zemsky, 1991, p. 5A)

Should Departments Change?

Enormous changes are coming for higher education, some of which we discuss in the following section: increased economic pressures, opportunities for collaboration with business and industry, the rise of new higher education providers, public concerns about student access and learning, the potential of technology to alter boundaries of time and space, the creation of a global network of information and commerce through the World Wide Web, shifting student demographics and attitudes, and changes in academic belief systems about learning and teaching. Such forces, say Inayatullah and Gidley (2000), will "bring new models of who teaches, who learns, and through what medium and through what organizational structures these people teach and learn" (p. 1).

 Academic departments will be at the center of the coming changes, and, despite their differences in size, culture, and mission, many departments will themselves need to change. Departments are crucial to all the core functions of a college or university—teaching, research, and service (Klein, 1985, p. 330; Pascarella and Terenzini, 1991, p. 614; Volkwein and Carbone, 1994; Willcoxson and Walter, 1995). As Zemsky (1995b) has said, "We are not going to restructure, reconfigure, re-anything this enterprise if we don't do it at the department level."

Current critiques (e.g., Kennedy, 1997, p. 277; Layzell, 1999) have wanted departments to:

- Improve undergraduate student learning, especially in general education;
- Collaborate across disciplines;
- Apply knowledge to community and workplace needs;
- Be more cost-efficient or "productive";
- Use technology to provide education by alternative means and transcend boundaries of time and space.

To achieve such change goals, reformers have suggested, for example, that departments undergo program review

(Mets, 1995), assess student learning (Banta, Lund, Black, and Oblander, 1996; Gardiner, 2000; Nichols, 1995a), or be made more responsible for their own financial bottom line (Adams, 1997; Whalen, 1991). In a survey, 37 provosts from public land-grant universities most frequently wanted departments to be more interdisciplinary, be more entrepreneurial, have strong leadership, and collaborate to promote institutional reform (Edwards, 1999). Throughout this monograph, we summarize such reform initiatives and relate them to the department's characteristics (see the appendix for a summary). Each reform initiative must build upon the sometimes highly varied characteristics of the departments involved.

Can Departments Change?

Becher and Kogan (1992) have described the department as "the most substantial barrier against externally imposed innovations, and one within whose protective walls the individual academic can most effectively shelter from any unwelcome winds of change" (p. 136). On the other hand, Seymour claims that "as the core of a decentralized, informalized, complex organization, the departmental unit has tremendous *potential* to initiate innovation" (1988, pp. 12–13, italics in original). Zemsky argues that "the department provides the very organizational structure needed to achieve a collective goal. It epitomizes the concept of the professional team, jointly responsible for the teaching and scholarship of its members" (1991, p. 5A).

We take the more hopeful view: Departments are not merely silos or barriers or dinosaurs; they are adapting organisms, trying to accomplish difficult and complex tasks in difficult and complex circumstances. It is not clear whether departments can change sufficiently to be effective in the rapidly changing world they face. But the only hope for change lies in building upon departments' own structures, cultures, and avenues of potential change.

How to Use This Volume

This volume addresses all who might propose change—department members, chairs, deans and provosts, scholars of higher education, state and national policymakers, consultants, and leaders of disciplinary and higher education associations. The scope of change may be national—concerned with "the" department—or local, as a department chair, members, or central administrators try to help a particular department fulfill its mission. We define change as a deliberate action intended to improve the department.

The literature suggests that there is no single recipe for change nor any single universal pattern of variables that affect change (Becher and Kogan, 1992; Toombs and Tierney, 1991). But writers such as Lucas (1994, pp. 54–59; 2000a), Angelo (2000), Gmelch and Miskin (1993, pp. 35–62), Senge, Roberts, and Ross (1994), and Senge (2000) propose sequences or guidelines that may be helpful. This volume supports four activities for practitioners who are planning change. Our four steps are not contradictory to those cited but rather are meant to enrich them with a perspective that places high importance on shaping strategies to the department's own characteristics.

1. Assess the pressures for change. Decide whether changes are needed.

2. Seek the greatest possible understanding of how departments work and how departmental structures and cultures suggest avenues for change. The literature on change in higher education strongly emphasizes that those who would instigate change must understand the culture (Bolman and Deal, 1991; Ewell, 1997; Lucas, 1994). The broadest definition of "culture" includes everything an organization is: its actions and structures as well as its values, beliefs, and rituals (Austin, 1994).

In our descriptions of the various aspects of departments, we integrate several different "frames" or ways of viewing organizations (Bensimon, Neumann, and Birnbaum, 1989; Bolman and Deal, 1991; Janzow, Hinni, and Johnson, 1996). Bolman and Deal describe frames as "both windows on the world and lenses that bring the world into focus" (1991, p. 11). This volume integrates the *symbolic* frame, which emphasizes the values, culture, myths, symbols, and rituals of an organization; the *structural* frame, which emphasizes the formal roles and relationships; the *human resource* frame, which focuses on tailoring the organization to its people; and the *political* frame, which views organizations as forums where units compete for power. Each frame offers valuable insights. Birnbaum holds that leaders (and, we would add, department members) in complex organizations need multiple frames and theories (1988, p. xvi).

We define change as a deliberate action intended to improve the department.

3. Implement a variety of change strategies adapted to the local situation. The appendix summarizes the main points we make about departments and the avenues for change that those characteristics suggest. Departments, however, differ widely. Further, the change literature emphasizes that long-lasting, effective change must take place across multiple fronts. A single program, such as teaching awards, a teaching and learning center, or training for chairs, if isolated, may not suffice to bring about long-lasting change (Ewell, 1997).

Thus, we expect that readers will use the sections in this monograph as a heuristic, to suggest ways of studying their own department and constructing an integrated set of change strategies. For example, suppose that the needed change is for the department to enhance undergraduate student learning. First, read the section on values, asking What are the values that affect how the department manages undergraduate student learning? Are there ways to work with, or change, those values? Then go on to the sections on disciplines, power, organization, leadership, and so on, asking What do these insights about departments suggest for helping this department to attend more carefully to student learning? Each section ends with questions for practitioners to aid in this inquiry process. Some departments will be quite different from those in the literature we summarize here, so readers may have to use our descriptions and questions suggestively, not prescriptively. Change strategies must arise from these understandings.

All the various change strategies we suggest in this monograph fall into six categories, which may be helpful in considering all of one's options for change: (a) change the environment; (b) change the type of person in the department; (c) address values; (d) change or build upon the way the department is structured in terms of its organization, its leadership positions, its reward systems, its dispersion of power, or its forums for conversation and decision making; (e) affect the decision-making process in which the department is engaged; (f) create alternative structures such as institutes or offices of first-year studies to take over some of the department's functions.

For example, a social science department in a research university participated in a self-study process that highlighted some aspects of its environment and its departmental culture and characteristics. The members became convinced that the department needed to pay more attention to undergraduate student learning. In the self-study, they saw that their department highly valued special disciplinary expertise and that everyone had an area of expertise, but that no one took the undergraduate introductory courses as an area of expertise. Thus, these courses were overlooked and minimized. They also saw that the department had a very short career ladder for faculty, especially those who specialized in teaching. Several of their senior faculty were stuck at the level of associate professor because promotion to full professor was based only on research. This fact was a strong message to new faculty about what really counted. The department members realized that they had few avenues for collecting information about their students' learning and satisfaction and that a significant percentage of their introductory students were transferring to the business college. Based on this study, they decided that, to enhance undergraduate student learning, they would (a) hire a tenure-track faculty member with special expertise in the pedagogy of the discipline whose task would be to restructure the introductory courses; (b) change the tenure guidelines to allow promotion to full professor on the basis of outstanding teaching combined with competent research; (c) hold exit interviews with graduating seniors and then feed that information back into departmental decision making about curriculum and pedagogy; and (d) join with departments in the business college to offer a joint undergraduate degree. They chose these particular strategies because of the characteristics of their department. In another case, a humanities department in a two-year college, after a self-study, focused on the large percentage of their students who were taught by adjuncts, the lack of rewards for the adjuncts, and the dissociation of the adjuncts from the department. They decided to try to enhance student learning by designating more carefully a set of rewards for teaching, including rewards for adjuncts, and by bringing adjuncts more fully into the collegial conversation about teaching—a strategy that fit their particular culture.

In neither of these cases did all department members want the change. And those who wanted it did not necessarily agree how to bring it about. Thus, the change strategies in part were chosen on the basis of what those who wanted the changes could actually accomplish.

In implementing change, the initial strategies may not be sufficient, or they may not be as effective as hoped. Change and the planning of change must be ongoing, with continual adaptation as the department learns what works. Above all, change must aim at what the department must *be* as well as what it must do.

4. Consider what the department should be. The overarching goal, beyond any particular change, is what the department wants to *be*. A department that functions in a healthy way can learn from its mistakes and can deal with the change agendas of tomorrow as well as those of today. A strand of visionary literature calls for departments to achieve "authentic collegiality" enhanced by "quality" concepts (Massy, Wilger, and Colbeck, 1994), to be a "team" (Ramsden, 1998; Wergin, 1994), to practice "collegial entrepreneurialism" (Clark, 2000), or to be a "learning" department (Angelo, 2000, Argyris and Schön, 1978; Brown, 1997; Heller, 1982; Rutherford, Fleming, and Mathias, 1985; Senge, 1996, 2000). Several traits are essential:

- *Self-knowledge:* Understanding their own and other cultures, environments, assumptions, values, and mental models;
- *Systems thinking:* Exploring and understanding how all elements of an organization and its environment interact;
- *Open, productive interaction:* Valuing greater closeness, more time together, more synergistic interaction, and healthy ways of managing conflict;
- *High freedom for individuals:* Emphasizing high freedom for individuals and valuing personal mastery;
- *Outward focus on environment, stakeholders, and results:* Evaluating the effects of the group's decisions so that group learning can take place;
- *Entrepreneurialism:* Valuing entrepreneurial and imaginative solutions born from interaction and commitment of the members of the group;
- *Fostering individuals' commitment to the well-being of the group;*
- *An emphasis on group and individual learning:* Changing behaviors on the basis of examination of the department's values and the outcomes of its work;
- *Gathering and acting on information about the department's culture and environment;*

- *Good leaders:* Supporting leaders who are open, collaborative, and strive for joint decisions, but also are proactive in guiding the department. The organization maximizes both formal and informal leadership. It helps individuals build leadership skills.

Observers have found few departments that match the vision (Massy, Wilger, and Colbeck, 1994; Wergin, 1994), though Clark (2000) points to certain institutions in other nations as exemplars. Our contention in this volume is that departments in the United States are still searching for viable notions of what to be. Such visions must be based on an understanding of departmental environments, values, structures, and cultures.

Angelo (2000) suggests guidelines for achieving a "learning" department:

1. *Build shared trust: Begin by lowering social and interpersonal barriers to change. . . .*
2. *Build shared motivation: Collectively determine goals worth working toward and problems worth solving—and consider the likely costs and benefits. . . .*
3. *Build a shared language: Develop a collective understanding of new concepts (mental models) needed for transformation. . . .*
4. *Design backward and work forward: Work backward from the shared vision and long-term goals to determine outcomes, strategies, and activities. . . .*
5. *Think and act systematically: Understand the advantages and limitations of the larger systems within which you operate and seek connections and applications to those larger worlds. . . .*
6. *Practice what you preach: Use what you have learned about individual and organizational learning to inform and explain your efforts and strategies. . . .*
7. *Do not assume, ask: Make the implicit explicit. Use assessment to focus on what matters most.* (pp. 80–86)

Our four steps can be integrated with Angelo's, and our suggestions will especially enrich guidelines 4 and 5 as department members and other change agents attempt to understand how the department works and to choose strategies based on the department's own characteristics.

Background for This Volume

Our analysis in this volume is based not only on our literature review and our experiences as faculty and administrators, but also on our involvement since 1991 as leaders of PIRT (Project to Improve and Reward Teaching) at the University of Cincinnati. Fifty-eight departments have volunteered to join this program, which helps them form and implement their own plans to enhance teaching and student learning. The PIRT office provides small amounts of funding, consulting for departments, resource materials, and regular interaction among member departments. Departmental actions have included weighing teaching more fully in promotion and tenure, providing increased recognition and rewards for teaching, hosting departmental workshops on teaching, assessing student learning, and increasing mentoring for teaching assistants (TAs) in their teaching roles (Carey, Soled, and Walvoord, 1998).

From 1991 to 1996, most of the coauthors of this volume collaborated to conduct a more focused qualitative study of change in eight PIRT departments. Data came from repeated interviews with selected department members over multiyear periods, examination of departmental documents, and observation of department meetings and other events. We bring also to this volume our long-term experiences as department members and leaders in various disciplines and types of institutions, as a university president, and as directors of university-wide programs such as general education, honors, and faculty development.

Departments differ widely. Not all need to change in the same ways, but our conviction is that departments in the future must change both in what they do and in what they become. That change will be complex and difficult. Departments must build upon their own particular qualities, structures, and cultures to fulfill their crucial roles.

Departments differ widely. Not all need to change in the same ways, but our conviction is that departments in the future must change both in what they do and in what they become.

ASSESSING THE PRESSURES FOR DEPARTMENTAL CHANGE

The first of four steps for change this volume supports is to assess the pressures for change. We mean assessment here to include the gathering and interpreting of information about the department's structures, outcomes, or environment for the purpose of improving the department. Pressures for change may come when the department sees that it is not prospering or not serving its mission effectively for its current constituencies, when old constituencies disappear or change their demands, or when new opportunities arise. The purpose of this section is to help departments in any of these situations.

National Pressures for Change in Higher Education

Not all departments face the same external pressures for change. The following paragraphs summarize some that operate nationally; each reader must assess his or her own department's situation.

Political and economic pressures

College costs to families have risen sharply in relation to family income as costs to colleges rise. Parents and students believe that colleges are expensive and wasteful (Goethals and Frantz, 1998; National Center for Education Statistics [NCES], 1996a, Table 37; 1997b; Institute for Research in Higher Education, 1997; Reisberg, 1998; Public Agenda and others, 2000).

Government funding for higher education has decreased (NCES, 1997c, 1998), offset by a significant rise in federal funding for research (NCES, 1998).

Publics are concerned about student learning, access, graduation, productivity, and faculty work (Anderson, 1992; Schmidt, 1998a, 1998b, 2000; Smith, 1990; Sykes, 1988; Zemsky, 1993).

Stakeholders demand collaboration with business and industry and flexible delivery of education (Schmidt, 1998a, 1998b).

New for-profits compete on the basis of cost, flexibility, and curricular relevance, and they experiment with new departmental and faculty roles (Marchese, 1998; Winston, 1999).

Accreditors, legislatures, and boards increasingly demand evidence of student learning (Dill, 1998; Green, 1997; Michael, 1998; Schmidt, 2000).

Technological advances

Beyond bricks and mortar and beyond the virtual university, visionaries imagine a "global learning infrastructure where millions of students interact with a vast array of individual and institutional suppliers . . . through multiple technologies including the Internet, broadband cable, and satellite" (Heterick, Mingle, and Twigg, 1997, p. 4). Some observers predict that technology will challenge the most basic assumptions behind traditional instruction (Privateer, 1999; see Bates [2000] for a discussion of technology issues for department chairs).

The student population

Student bodies increasingly are female, part time, minority, and older than traditional college age (NCES, 1996b, 1997a, 1998).

Students' reasons for attending school

The percentage of students who view "developing a meaningful philosophy of life" as essential or very important has sharply declined (Astin, 1998).

Students' expectations and attitudes

Contemporary students may view education as a product to be purchased, insist on quality, have only a temporary and provisional commitment, and see little need to spend time on campus beyond class contact hours (Levine and Cureton, 1998). They are more individualistic: They want their own dorm room, and they do not socialize in large groups as much as previous generations (Levine and Cureton, 1998). They desire personal growth and creativity (O'Connell, 1998). They are also technoliterate (Plater, 1995; Green and Gilbert, 1995).

The academic belief system

Educational concerns, beliefs, and processes are being reexamined:

- *From a teaching to a learning paradigm:* The pedagogical field is constantly infused with new disciplinary insights, such as those from neuroscience (Marchese, 1998). The historically dominant instructional paradigm is slowly being replaced by a learning paradigm (Barr and Tagg, 1995) in which learning outcomes matter more than inputs. Reformers call for more active and collaborative learning.

- *Flexible time and space:* New technologies allow transcendence of the boundaries of time and space that led to the current structure of higher education. Reformers question whether education should rely any longer on credit hours as the measure of education (Ewell, 1998; Guskin, 1994; Plater, 1995).

- *Emphasis on interdisciplinary knowledge:* The need for multidisciplinary approaches to societal problems encourages aggregations of disciplines into multidisciplinary institutes and, as well, increasing fragmentation within disciplines as researchers adopt new and diverse modes of inquiry (Plater, 1995).

What do these pressures imply for departments nationally?

The pressures we have described lie behind the five demands for change we summarized in the introductory section: (a) improve undergraduate education, (b) collaborate across disciplines, (c) apply knowledge to community and workplace needs, (d) be more cost-efficient, and (e) use technology to provide education by alternative means. In addition, the department in a free society must protect core values, freely pursue knowledge, and question society's mores. It must balance the loudest demands with those not currently in the public eye, such as pure research. It must position itself to respond to the next round of demands. It must make faculty life rewarding and enticing for the next generation that will have to staff higher education.

The Need for Assessment of Outcomes

External constituents are demanding not only that departments *say* they are doing good things and not only that they measure *how hard they are trying,* but also that they *measure outcomes.* Further, departments themselves, if they are to use their resources most efficiently to serve their missions, need information about the outcomes of their efforts. Gone are the days when it would suffice to assume that all the work on inputs such as curriculum, hiring, teaching, and budget allocation must certainly be producing the outcomes hoped for.

Implications for Change

Departments differ widely. Not all need to change in the same ways, but in an environment so volatile and so demanding, most departments may have to do things differently and be something different. Assessment of the environment and outcomes helps the department to decide what changes are needed.

Read the departmental environment

The wise practitioner will ask how the department gets its information about the national and regional environment. For example, is someone in the department reading and reporting information from such national sources as *The Chronicle of Higher Education, Educause,* the Pew Roundtable, and listservs such as that maintained by the TLT Group (aahesgit@list.cren.net)? Is someone bringing back information from national conferences and national journals? Is someone watching trends in relevant granting agencies and in the state legislature and the board of trustees? What do the institution's own president and offices of development, public relations, and institutional research know about the environment, and how is the department getting and using that information? How is all this information integrated, discussed, and acted on within the department? What further information does the department need about the environment or about the department's success in serving its rapidly changing world?

In addition to ongoing reports, a department might consider a retreat or strategic planning session. For example, a German department with which we have worked faced the imminent retirement of a cohort of faculty who had brought the department into the top ranks of reputation in research. The department had not been allowed to rehire enough top research faculty to replace them. Further, the environment was changing in other significant ways, including new institutional resources devoted to undergraduate student learning, which the department had largely routinized and placed in the hands of adjunct professors and graduate TAs. To help the department examine its environment and decide on a new mission, structures, and strategies, the chair engaged Walvoord, an outside consultant, to lead a daylong retreat. Walvoord adapted a retreat model described by Schein (1992). She asked the department to name the various "pots" from which it received resources or reputation—for example, granting agencies, publications, undergraduate language requirements, and so on. Then small groups of department members generated, for each of these pots, what the department had to do to achieve those resources and how the resources themselves were changing. They wrote all this information on newsprint sheets and taped the sheets to the walls of the room. Then, literally surrounded by their environment, they assessed their situation. Alarm—the outcome the chair had wanted—led to plans for change to place more emphasis on undergraduate student learning. Such plans require further assessment— gathering specific data on undergraduate learning, exploring best practices in other language departments, and scanning the environment more carefully—but the one-day retreat got the process started and catapulted department members' thinking to new realms.

The German department began with the "frame" of the department as a resource/reputation-seeking entity. Alternatively, using the frame of the department as a mission-driven enterprise, one may start with mission, then goals, then strategies. Missions explain what the department does, for whom, and what its focus is. Goals are targets relating to key indicators of departmental success derived from the mission. For example, a department may establish as its goal that it place 30% of its graduates in the top ten firms in its field. Strategies are the means by which the goals are achieved. When mission and goals have been defined, the department can ask, "How is our mission served or undermined by our reward system? By our organizational structure? Our recruitment and socialization of new faculty?" And so on. Again, this assessment integrates analysis of the external pressures, the department's strategies, and outcomes such as student learning, national reputation, income from grants, and the like. Diamond (1993, 1999) outlines a mission-driven process of planning for change.

Assess outcomes
In addition to reading its external environment, a "learning" department must assess its outcomes and determine how its structures and strategies help it to fulfill its mission. An extensive how-to literature addresses this process. Especially useful are Gardiner (2000) for an overview of the assessment

of educational effectiveness and Nichols (1995a, 1995b, 1995c) for extensive how-to guides. Tobias (1995) has formulated a set of review questions explicitly designed to help the department focus on the experiences of its undergraduate students. Banta, Lund, Black, and Oblander (1996) provide examples of departmental assessment practice. Watch for new materials from the American Association for Higher Education, from regional and disciplinary accrediting agencies, ongoing issues of *Assessment Update* (http://www.josseybass.com), and proceedings of conferences such as AAHE's annual conference on assessment (http://www.aahe.org) and the annual national Indianapolis Assessment Conference (http://www.hoosiers. iupui.edu/paiimain/conferen.htm). Other assessment resources are listed in Gardiner, Anderson, and Cambridge (1997).

Once the department members and/or external change agents have considered what sorts of change are needed, they must continue their exploration of how the department's own structures and cultures suggest strategies for change. Such exploration is the task of the next sections.

EXAMINING VALUES IN THE DEPARTMENT

The president of a prominent Catholic research university offers the theology department a new faculty line position to be filled by a noted theologian/priest whom the president, himself a theologian, wants to place on the faculty. The department refuses. Members of a mathematics department are in deep disagreement over whether to adopt a new calculus pedagogy. The side favoring the new methods believes it has a majority, but it declines to bring the matter to a departmental vote because, as its leading proponent explains, "The vote would split the department." Each of these actions reveals underlying values.

This section begins the second step of planning for change: understanding how departmental characteristics themselves suggest strategies for change. It also focuses on one of the frames mentioned in the introductory section—the "symbolic" frame that emphasizes the role of symbols, myths, values, and culture. As Kennedy (1997) says, "The fact that most institutional decisions represent, in the end, the collective values and aspirations of the faculty helps to explain why universities are organized the way they are and behave as they do" (p. 23). Those who plan for change must understand departmental values.

Five Core Academic Values
Exploring one's own department's values might start with a consideration of five values about which there is widespread agreement in the literature (Kuh and Whitt, 1988; Lane, 1985, p. 247; Ruscio, 1987b) and that seem especially important in planning for change. Ask whether your department holds these values and in what ways or whether it differs.

Collegiality
Baldridge, Curtis, Ecker, and Riley (1991) note that the literature on collegiality contains several strands: (a) collegial decision making that includes wide faculty participation and consensus; (b) the basis of collegiality in professional specialization of faculty members who need freedom from bureaucratic constraints and who function as a company of equals; and (c) the utopian prescription that focuses on connectedness and community, humane ways of dealing with others, and human development as a goal. "Departmental Organization, Decision Making, and

Interaction" further explores the organizational structures that derive from collegiality.

Autonomy

Both autonomy and academic freedom are expressions of the "deep-seated belief among academics that worthwhile intellectual activity cannot survive in a context in which outside demands begin to exercise a dominating influence over choice and action" (Becher and Kogan, 1992, p. 101). Personal autonomy is consistently found to be one of the main sources of faculty job satisfaction (Pollicino, 1996) and an object of departmental action (Epstein, 1974). Departmental autonomy was the chief value at stake in our earlier example of the theology department that turned down a faculty position.

Academic freedom

The American Association of University Professors (1995) has defined academic freedom as the right of the academic to express scholarly judgments within his or her area of expertise, whether in the classroom or as a citizen. Academic freedom is often invoked by faculty to support broader autonomies, however (Edwards, 1993, p. 16; Dill, 1992, p. 56). For example, at the University of Cincinnati in the 1990s, a university-wide reform required that faculty submit their general education course plans to a faculty committee that would decide whether the course met the requirements. Academic freedom was often invoked by faculty who argued against the whole idea and also by individual faculty when their course proposals were critiqued or turned down by the committee. Faculty notions of academic freedom thus arise from, and bolster, the high value that faculty place on freedom of choice and action in pedagogy as well as in research.

Specialization/expertise

Faculty and departments gain their credibility and authority on the basis of their specialized expertise (Bergquist, 1992). Expertise, then, becomes the basis of collegiality, autonomy, and academic freedom. And though race, gender, and other biases may be at work, academic expertise is the espoused basis for hiring, rank, prestige, and pay.

Reason and the scientific method

Many observers have noted the hegemony of reason as the foundation of knowledge construction and as the ideal for behavior in the academy (Louis, Anderson, and Rosenberg, 1995, p. 397). The scientific method is one instantiation of reason. Contemporary scholars have attacked the presumption that scientific knowledge is true or objective in any final sense and have emphasized the social dimensions that shape the construction of knowledge (Karseth, 1995). Nonetheless, for much of academic life and practice, the scientific method still forms a point of reference, either for acceptance or rejection. The assumption that educated minds in collegial deliberation will reach consensus is itself based on a fundamental trust in reason.

The missing values?

The literature we have just reviewed may be ignoring some core values, especially, it seems to us, the value of service and of mentoring. There may be other values that the reader's own department holds. It is important to identify the core values in one's own situation. In the final part of the section, we suggest some sources and strategies that may help departments to identify their own values.

Though widely shared, interdependent, and overlapping, the five values in practice may conflict.

Departmental values guide behavior, structure, aspirations, and rewards within departments. Change in departments will have to be built from, around, or in spite of departmental values. Resistance to change will arise as the values are challenged (Schein, 1992). But values are not simple. The tensions that arise around values may be as important for change as the values themselves.

Values May Not Work Rationally or Consistently

Argyris and Schön make a useful distinction between the theories or values that people espouse and the theories and values that shape people's actual practice (Argyris, 1982a, 1982b; Argyris and Schön, 1978). For example, faculty in a department may say that they value collegiality, but a new faculty member finds that no one drops by her office to talk.

Though widely shared, interdependent, and overlapping, the five values in practice may conflict. For example, Weick (1983) notes that the traditional scientific demands of validity, objectivity, and accuracy urge individuals not to be co-opted by the thinking and perspectives of the group, but the tradition of collegiality and the demands of common goals urge cohesive, collective effort. Thus, "the strange organizational arrangements found in universities can be understood as emergent structures that incorporate a basic ambivalence" toward these two values (p. 253).

Coexisting Cultures and Values

To adopt a cultural perspective means in part, say Rhoads and Tierney, "recognizing the variety of institutional sub-cultures" (1992, p. 5). Value differences may occur along lines of discipline, rank, status, race, gender, sexual prefer-ence, or age. Further, the conflicting cultural values of ad-ministrators and faculty (Peterson and White, 1992; Schoenfeld, 1994) can make administratively derived mis-sions and reforms unacceptable or incomprehensible to faculty.

Bergquist (1992) identifies four different "cultures" that coexist in many institutions, though one or the other may be dominant: the collegial culture, the managerial culture, the negotiating culture, and the developmental culture. Bergquist's case study of "Peter Armantrout" depicts "Fairfield College" as a traditional collegial culture that "em-phasizes and rewards informal and quasi-political collabora-tion among faculty, as well as independent research and scholarship" (p. 9). It epitomizes the five core academic values. At the same time, at Fairfield, the "managerial cul-ture" is emerging, spurred by external pressures for account-ability and by the increasing professionalization of adminis-trators. The managerial culture "values efficient and effective educational programming" and "attempts to assess the extent to which specific objectives are being achieved"—a set of values that the collegial culture views as "intrusive and offensive" (p. 10). In response to the managerial culture, the "negotiating culture" arises, expressed as Armantrout participates in union organization and leadership at Fairfield. In the negotiating culture, "faculty members perceive their relationship to the administration as primarily adversarial and define their work via formal contractual processes rather than the more informal methods used in the other three cultures" (p. 11). Also coexistent at Fairfield College is the "developmental culture," expressed through faculty development workshops, programs that focus on student learning and development, and the like. In that culture, "emphasis is placed on the careful, collaborative assessment of current campus resources and impending campus needs and the formulation of comprehensive strategies for meeting those needs" (p. 12). Criteria for assessment "often concern student growth and development (stages of student development or the acquisition of critical thinking skills) or faculty development (levels of faculty morale or student suggestions regarding instructional improvement)" (p. 12).

Though Bergquist (1992) describes the four subcultures as coexisting, there is an underlying chronological movement in his scheme. The traditional values embedded in what he calls the "collegial" culture have been increasingly challenged by external pressures: increases in size and complexity resulting in greater bureaucracy, greater specialization in the disciplines, political pressures, economic realities, and technological advances, to name a few. Currently, coexisting cultures appear to be quite common in institutions of higher education (Cameron and Ettington, 1988, pp. 386–388; Smart, Kuh, and Tierney, 1997; Smart and St. John, 1996). This volume views departments not as dinosaurs, but as living entities struggling to protect traditional collegial values but also to adapt to a rapidly changing world.

Implications for Change
Several possible implications for change emerge from a consideration of the core academic values in all their complexity and of the forces that challenge them and coexist with them.

Examine the department's own values
Examination of values, and more broadly of culture, lies at the core of the notion of the "learning organization." Says Schein (1992), "The essence of [the] learning process will be to give organizational culture its due" (p. 392). Heller (1982) analyzes how a language department might clarify what he calls its "theory-of-action"—that is, its understanding of the underlying causes of a problem (p. 13). Bare (1980), Bolton and Boyer (1973), Crockett (1973), Hewton (1982), Kressel, Bailey, and Forman (1999), Schein (1992), and Smith, Scholten, Russell, and McCormack (1997) also describe strategies for departmental self-study.

Look for common values in different guises

Bergquist's scheme of named "cultures" (1992) is very useful, but it also obscures some of the shared values among cultures. For example, the collegial values of reason and disciplinary work based on data share common ground with the managerial focus on gathering evidence about outcomes. The value of nurturing students, ascribed to the developmental culture, has its echoes in each of the other subcultures. These similarities may provide a basis for dialogue and change.

Analyze how values affect change

In planning change, one might analyze how the culture's values may operate. For example, Chaffee and Sherr (1992) analyze how traditional faculty values will both support and inhibit faculty members' interest in teaching within the Total Quality Management framework. Wergin (1994) does the same for the concept of departments as "teams."

Build on the values

Values do not in themselves preclude change. Gmelch (1995), giving advice to chairs about how to manage departmental conflict, recommends "[capturing] the energy from autonomy and synergistically [transforming] it into productive ideas for the department" (pp. 37–38). A major theme of this volume is that change can and must be built on the value of autonomy.

Another example, this time of building on the value of specialization: A research-oriented economics department known to us recently hired a new kind of specialist—a faculty member whose primary task was to revise the introductory course and to focus on pedagogy in the discipline. She followed a disciplinary specialist's pattern—got a large grant to revise the course, published her research on student learning outcomes in that course—and received tenure (though not without some conflict within the department about whether disciplinary pedagogy could be a legitimate specialty). Extending the notion of specialization to include heretofore neglected or newly expanded departmental tasks worked for change in this case.

Change the values

Cultures and their values do change over time (Cameron and Ettington, 1988, pp. 386–388). But can reformers deliberately change values? Only slowly and by indirect measures, observers agree. Easterby-Smith argues:

> *The danger is that if one simply attacks the existing values of an organisation—say those of scholarship, colleagueship and individual freedom—one runs the risk of destroying individuals' sense of purpose, and thus creating a highly demoralised organisation. If values are to be shifted, say towards a greater commercial orientation—then they must be done in a way which allows for retention of the original values in parallel. It is a kind of bridging idea that is needed. This will take time, and not a little creativity.* (1987, p. 51)

The notion of "in parallel" is important; a common mode of change in higher education is not to kill something but rather to encourage alternative patterns and structures to grow up beside it. Schein (1992) discusses an organization's need for pilot experiments with new "assumptions."

Redefine the values

Values, though they keep the same names, may change meaning over time. For example, we have already noted that "academic freedom" has extended in application. One can try to stem such changes, but another strategy for change is to *encourage* redefinition of a traditional value. For example, one department in a small, open-admissions two-year college known to us comprised a core of tenured faculty plus twice as many adjuncts. In the Good Old Days, collegiality meant that faculty meetings were set, everyone was invited, and decisions were made by consensus. Rich, informal exchange was created as faculty met one another daily in the hallways and classrooms. As the number of part-time faculty increased, however, these modes no longer resulted in collegial governance. Adjuncts could not make daytime meetings, did not have offices, and often scarcely knew one another or the full-time faculty. In an attempt to accommodate both groups, the department decided to hold its meetings at 5 P.M. Now nobody could come. So the department set up myriad meetings of small groups of full- and part-time faculty.

Representatives from the small groups then reported back to the leadership group, which now expanded to include some part-time as well as full-time faculty. This "cell" model worked better. The expansion of collegial modes beyond the old-fashioned town meeting style allowed this department to expand and adapt its definition of collegiality and its ways of maintaining that important value. A major conclusion of this volume is that departments must invent creative new modes of collegiality, as contemporary conditions make traditional forms difficult.

Strengthen subcultures

Leaders might look for ways to enhance the power and influence of subcultures that hold desired values. An example is a foundation studies program in a school of design known to us. Its faculty taught first- and second-year students bound for design, art, and architecture. These faculty, keenly interested in first- and second-year students' learning, were also highly experimental and open to computer applications. Historically treated as low status and underfunded, these faculty, with the dean's encouragement, began to take the lead in developing computer-based design courses. Their cutting-edge expertise allowed them to garner more faculty positions, greater prestige, more courses, and higher visibility. Despite significant opposition from some faculty, this group of computer designers was successful in establishing an undergraduate major in computer-aided design—an important future direction for the school. The dean, by supporting them, found an avenue for innovation amid a hitherto low-status subculture. Schein (1992) emphasizes the encouragement or suppression of subcultures as one of the major tasks of leaders in mature organizations.

Departments must invent creative new modes of collegiality, as contemporary conditions make traditional forms difficult.

Questions for Practitioners

- What values are at work in shaping how these departments think and act? Do espoused values differ from those actually being used?
- Can we argue that change is needed to reestablish or fully realize the values?
- Are people ready to change the values?
- Can we redefine the values?
- Where are subcultures that embody the values we want, and can they be strengthened?

- Is there common ground among seemingly conflicting values? Are there invisible values that can help move the department forward?

These questions and the strategies that arise from them must then be integrated with strategies aimed at other aspects of departmental life, as discussed later.

THE DISCIPLINE AND THE DEPARTMENT

The disciplinary basis of departments has been held responsible for some of their faults—particularly overspecialization (Costanza, 1990), inattention to the integrative demands of general education (Lattuca and Stark, 1994), and inability to form cross-disciplinary collaborations to address society's most pressing problems (Toombs and Escala, 1987, p. 13).

Yet the discipline is the foundation of specialization—one of the five core academic values. Disciplinary specialization is an important basis for other values, particularly autonomy and academic freedom. Because faculty are experts in their fields, they can claim that only peers in the field can accurately judge their work (Baldridge, 1971). Because of their role in advancing disciplinary knowledge, they must be free of external interference. By disciplinary connections, they enhance their autonomy from the university (Alpert, 1986). In universities, research suggests that many faculty feel greater commitment to the discipline than to the department or the institution (Boyer, 1990). Through contributions to disciplinary knowledge, departments maintain their national rankings, gain reputations, and draw top-ranking faculty and graduate students, thus enhancing their power both outside and inside the institution (Becher and Kogan, 1992; Dill, 1984; Webster and Skinner, 1996).

To suggest that subunits be organized not by discipline but by function or some other principle (e.g., Armajani, Heydinger, and Hutchinson, 1994) is to challenge powerful values and benefits for both faculty and departments. Further, disciplinary organization points to the preeminence of knowledge-making as the focus of higher education. Clark (1987) views the department as the place where the discipline and the "enterprise" meet. We suggest an even more dynamic mediating function: A department at its best is the flexible belt, not the rigid cog, that translates intellectual knowledge into multiple kinds of service to multiple constituencies.

A department at its best is the flexible belt, not the rigid cog, that translates intellectual knowledge into multiple kinds of service to multiple constituencies.

Interdisciplinarity

A discipline is a set of assumptions and tools for viewing the world in a certain way, addressing certain kinds of questions, and valuing certain kinds of evidence and insight. Disciplines are not stable; they splinter into subdisciplines, and they combine with other disciplines. Among the great challenges to departments today are to keep up with the development of new subdisciplines, to participate with other disciplines in providing integrative education for undergraduate students, and to collaborate for interdisciplinary approaches to real-world problems. Such combinations may be very difficult because department members themselves were not interdisciplinary in their training or because the assumptions, values, and tools of various disciplines may not easily mesh.

Differences Among the Disciplines

Despite the collaborations they might form, the physics department remains quite different from the psychology department—a fact that will influence departmental change. A substantial body of research has established that departments differ by a quality variously titled "paradigm development in the field," "consensus among members about their disciplinary methodology," or "the level of codification of the discipline's knowledge and method" (Braxton and Hargens, 1996). Researchers have found more than 70 variables related to this factor (Biglan, 1973a, 1973b; Bresser, 1984; Dahlgren and Pramling, 1985; Smart and Elton, 1982; Stoecker, 1993). Among them are concepts of learning and knowing, department members' educational values, teaching style/methods, teachers' tendency to involve students in the conduct of the course, time spent on teaching, the mix of teaching and research (Austin, 1996), the departmental faculty's involvement in teaching, emphasis by the chair on research and on graduate education, types of scholarly output generated, types of funding sources used, and attitudes of faculty (liberal or conservative political views, unified or diversified views of scholarly research and of "good" scholarship, and greater or lesser concern with the application of knowledge).

Faculty in humanities and social sciences tend to spend more time on teaching, have higher orientation and interest toward teaching, and more strongly emphasize student development, the goals of general education, active learning, and students' oral and writing skills. They differ from faculty in mathematics, science, and technical fields in their teaching methods and in the role the student plays in the classroom (Stark and Lattuca, 1997, pp. 216–217).

Though institutional type and size, departmental size and mission, highest degree granted, and other variables have been found to influence departmental characteristics (Braxton and Hargens, 1996, p. 36; Carroll and Gmelch, 1992; Groner, 1978; Hayward, 1986; Huber, 1994; Jordan, Meador, and Walters, 1989), it is clear that the discipline fundamentally affects the department.

Multiple Avenues for Disciplinary Influence on the Department

The discipline influences the department through multiple avenues that affect change.

- *The disciplinary association:* As Clark (1987) points out, disciplinary associations offer membership for faculty within a national or international community with shared goals and interests that may be different from the goals and interests of the institution.
- *Disciplinary values and norms:* The discipline is not only a disciplinary society, a body of knowledge, and a methodology. It is also a set of values and norms maintained by a community of faculty who find their identity within the discipline and who enact and transmit its values within their institutions and departments as they hire and promote new faculty, organize their work, make decisions, and shape their students' learning.
- *Hiring:* Theories by Holland (1973) suggest that faculty choose a discipline because of their own personality traits, thus influencing the types of people who will turn up in the hiring pool. Further, the discipline influences the hiring process through its societies, journals, networks of colleagues, and systems for generating recommendations by experts in the field (Burke, 1995; Smelser and Content, 1980, p. 157).
- *Socialization:* The graduate school may be focused very heavily on disciplinary agendas. Thus, when the new Ph.D. arrives at St. Hibiscus College or at AnyState University, considerable *disciplinary* socialization has already taken place, but socialization to the teaching, service, and governance responsibilities in a teaching-oriented college or university may barely have begun. Further, the forces that make all colleges and universities want to copy the model of the high-status institutions (Astin, 1985, 1993) will encourage St. Hibiscus or AnyState itself to become an arm of disciplinary

socialization, requiring that the faculty member publish in the discipline, thus encouraging the new faculty member to form further socializing connections with disciplinary societies, colleagues, mentors, journals, and presses.

- *Gatekeeping and evaluation:* Disciplines exert strong gatekeeping and evaluative influence through the disciplinary journals, discipline-based accreditation, the use of disciplinary peers for external review of a department, and national rankings of departments (Machung, 1998).

Implications for Change
Work with disciplinary differences
Disciplinary differences appear when departments are changing. Finnegan and Gamson's case study of four New England comprehensive universities and colleges (1996) illustrates the quite different ways in which mathematics departments and English departments adopted a research emphasis for their departments' missions. The change was influenced by "the nature and current discourse in the disciplines, departmental cohesion, departmental collective action, and congruence of goals between the department and the institution" (p. 171). Mathematics departments had more internal cohesiveness and acted more collectively with other departments to bring about the change. Change agents, then, must ask how the differences in disciplines will affect departmental change.

Change the disciplinary society
Because the disciplinary association is a visible locus of the discipline, several reform efforts have focused on it. For example, a Syracuse University project sponsored by the Pew Charitable Trusts, the Fund for the Improvement of Postsecondary Education, and the Lilly Endowment worked with disciplinary societies to construct a definition of "scholarship," attempting to get the disciplines formally to acknowledge teaching as scholarly work worthy of high status (Diamond and Adam, 1995, 2000). The Carnegie Project for the Scholarship of Teaching and Learning is also working with disciplinary societies (www.CarnegieFoundation.org).

Change criteria for rankings and review

Reformers also suggest changing the criteria for national rankings and for departmental review. To do that, new evaluation instruments are needed. The Carnegie Foundation for the Advancement of Teaching and the Pew Forum on Undergraduate Learning are supporting a National Survey of Student Engagement (NSSE), a questionnaire that measures such marks of engagement as how often students have talked to a professor outside of class. NSSE's goal is to provide an instrument that can be used for national rankings of institutions and departments to balance the emphasis on published research and grants (Ewell, 1999; www.indiana.edu/~nsse).

Strengthen institutional influence

Another approach is to strengthen institutional influence, in order to counterbalance disciplinary influence—an approach that depends on strategies discussed in a later section on departmental autonomy and power within the institution.

Change the disciplinary hiring pool

Bess (1990) says that current faculty are "miscast professionals" (p. 21) and suggests a new incentive structure to bring into the universities people who have genuine potential for being good teachers but who do not now see university teaching as a viable career. Diversity in gender, religion, ethnic background, and other traits may help to broaden the personality types found in a departmental hiring pool. Spelling out in the hiring process the department's expectations about a new faculty member's role might encourage applicants with desired traits.

Increasing the numbers or power of adjuncts and other nontraditional faculty who have looser ties to the disciplinary culture is another avenue for change. At the University of Phoenix, the faculty comprises almost entirely adjuncts, often without traditional degrees or publication and grant records, who teach from their professional expertise and whose primarily loyalty is to the institution, the students, and the profession rather than to research in the discipline (Traub, 1997).

To help teaching-oriented colleges and universities get a head start on socialization, many institutions have begun to pay more attention to training graduate students for teaching roles. A national initiative is the Pew-sponsored Preparing Future Faculty Project, which provides doctoral candidates with mentored experiences in teaching-oriented colleges and universities and which in 1999 launched projects that work specifically with departments in certain disciplines (www.preparing-faculty.org).

Encourage interdisciplinary collaboration

Structures that encourage interdisciplinary collaboration are another road to change. In one unionized research university, a collaboration between a physicist and a philosopher, which resulted in a publication, arose when the two faculty members began talking on the picket line during a faculty strike. The lesson: create such dialogue in other ways. At Whitworth College in Spokane, faculty for years have worked on interdisciplinary teams to plan and teach the integrative undergraduate core courses, resisting the temptation merely to divide the subject matter into disciplinary segments. A number of visits by Walvoord over 11 years have revealed their remarkable interdisciplinary sensibility and their attention to the needs of undergraduates.

Create alternative structures

Another reform effort tries to provide discipline-like societies, conferences, and journals for faculty (e.g., the National Association of Biology Teachers, www.nabt.org), or the interdisciplinary International Alliance of Teacher Scholars, www.iats.com). Journals are disciplinary (e.g., *Engineering Education*) and multidisciplinary (e.g., *Journal of Teaching Excellence*). Weimer's review of them (1993) notes that they did not meet the same standards for evidence and literature review as the top journals that publish disciplinary scholarship. Her review reveals much about the current higher education scene—ambiguity about standards for teaching expertise and research, about the basis of a publishing teacher's authority, about status in the profession, and about what constitutes evidence in teaching—a field where some of the most valuable knowledge exists as practitioner lore. Reformers might try to raise the quality of such journals by aping the standards applied to research in the discipline, or they might judge those standards inappropriate and seek to establish new ones.

Another role for alternative structures is to relieve the department of those tasks that its disciplinary organization makes difficult. For example, first-year studies offices, learning communities, and the kinds of theme-based units tried at Buffalo long ago (Levine, 1980) all attempt to provide a different locus for integration of learning among undergraduate students. Institutes try to foster interdisciplinary scholarship. Clark (2000) suggests that the university of the future needs to include both disciplinary departments that themselves become more entrepreneurial and collegial than at present, and loosely connected peripheral units that can reach across boundaries and link with a wide variety of other units. A related view is the model of the university as "core and cloud" (David, 1997; see also Zemsky and Massy, 1995), in which multiple kinds of loosely connected units surround the university's core, carrying out multiple tasks and collaborating with multiple stakeholders.

Build the "learning department"

This overview reveals that the impetus for change has arisen largely external to departments and has therefore used the avenues open to external change agents: increase external pressures, change the disciplinary societies and the criteria for ranking and review, give the department differently socialized new faculty, or establish alternative structures. Given the multiple avenues through which the discipline influences the department, however, it may be that the only hope of real change lies in the "learning" department to candidly examining its own relations to the discipline and its disciplinary values, and making changes it perceives are needed. Interestingly, Carnegie survey data suggest that at selective liberal arts colleges, research is more individualistic than bureaucratic and that faculty are often critical of their disciplines as narrow and irrelevant (Ruscio, 1987a). Perhaps with the greater collegiate loyalty that characterizes them, these faculty are already critically examining the claims on them of disciplinary work.

Questions for Practitioners

- How does the discipline influence the department(s) in our setting?
- What avenues are already operating for interdisciplinary

conversation and collaboration? What additional avenues might be possible and helpful?

- Would it be useful for our departments to become involved in one of the national initiatives that promote interdisciplinarity?
- Are there ways to strengthen department members' loyalty to the institution?
- How might department members be led to critically examine the role of the discipline in their values and actions?
- Is our hiring process promoting interdisciplinary collaboration?
- What structures already exist in the institution to help departments with those tasks that disciplinarity makes difficult? What structures might be formed?

In sum, the department is the expression of the academy's focus on knowledge. At its best, it translates intellectual energy into multiple kinds of service to multiple constituencies. Those who desire change in departments must choose change strategies that deal with disciplinary influences, integrating them with strategies we examine in the coming sections.

DEPARTMENTAL RELATIONS WITH
CENTRAL ADMINISTRATION

Describing how a central administration at a research university initiated departmental program review to encourage departmental accountability and change, Lincoln (1986) writes:

> *A . . . problem . . . has to do with the departments who unilaterally decide that they are "too busy" to enter into the program review process, or that they have too many problems at the moment to undergo review, [or] that a concurrent accreditation is taking too much of their time, or the like. . . . When an academic department refuses to admit the review committee and announces its intention to subvert the process, the response tends to be one of bafflement and confusion. The resolution of this recalcitrance awaits a more ingenious mind.*
> (pp. 16–17)

The department is not merely a subunit, obeying directives from above. Rather, it is a uniquely *autonomous* and *powerful* yet also uniquely *interdependent* structure within a very complex system, including the institution's culture, other departments, student services, the union, and other forces with which departments interact. We have chosen to focus this section on central administration because it plays a crucial role, but the wider context must be analyzed in any change plan.

This section draws primarily on the political frame, attending to dynamics of power, autonomy, and resources. But at its end, it suggests a broader view. The section speaks to those inside the department as well as central administrators (including deans of colleges) and others who support change from the outside. Departments and institutions differ widely. Each reader must analyze how autonomy and power operate in his or her own situation, using our descriptions as a heuristic guide.

Sources of Departmental Autonomy and Power

It is important for change agents to analyze the sources of departmental autonomy (the ability to determine one's own actions) and power (the ability to influence others), whatever they may be in the individual situation. Departmental power and autonomy may be enhanced by the following factors:

- *Academic values:* Autonomy is one of the five core academic values we have described. Epstein (1974) notes that "in the department, more than in business and government, the drive for self-governance has been effectively institutionalized" (p. 128).
- *The discipline:* The department uses the discipline to enhance its autonomy and power in relation to the central administration, as we described earlier. The saying about Atlas comes to mind: that he could lift the world if he had a place to stand on. The discipline gives the department a ground for its autonomy in relation to the central administration.
- *Departmental tasks:* The complexity of the department's tasks, as well as the expertise and judgment they require, make it difficult to control faculty or departmental actions by close surveillance or bureaucratic regulations (Baldridge, 1971).
- *Overlapping faculty networks:* As Baldridge (1971) has observed, universities and colleges often have a "parallel" governance structure in which faculty members exert influence up and down the hierarchy. Thus, a department may have one or more of its members serving as a faculty representative on the board of trustees, on a university planning committee that the provost has organized, on the curriculum committee, in the faculty senate, or in union activities. This notion of overlapping and intersecting networks provides a different perspective from the image some critics employ, of departments as autonomous fiefdoms, each behind its own wall. A map of departmental networks might look like a map of medieval Europe, in which city-states have walls but are situated critically on waterways, mountain passes, and roads that bring oriental spices and new ideas.
- *Selection of members and chair:* Departments typically exercise strong control over hiring and socializing their own faculty and choosing their own chair. In some departments, the chair tends to be seen as first among equals and to envision his or her role as protecting the interests of the department against centralized incursions (Becher and Kogan, 1992).
- *Independent income:* A study by Salancik and Pfeffer (1974) demonstrated that departments that could best

obtain *external* resources for the organization (grants, contracts, graduate students) could also best obtain *internal* resources within the organization. Research universities typically return to the department a percentage of the unrestricted funds from the granting agency. The university does so as an incentive, because it needs its departments to attract grants. Ironically, it thereby enhances the autonomy and power of those departments.

Departmental Autonomy Does Not Preclude Change

Because the department enjoys considerable autonomy through all the forces described above, change must arise from a respect for that autonomy and must build upon it. Let us examine again Lincoln's case study (1986), quoted at the beginning of this section. From the top, departments' refusal looks like resistance to change. "Recalcitrance" is the term Lincoln gives it. But examine more closely the reasons the departments gave for not participating: They were undergoing accreditation review, they were too busy, they had too many problems. Another way to read these responses is that the department is itself struggling with multiple forces that are demanding effort and change. It is setting its own priorities and trying to use wisely its resources of time and attention. Central administration, says Levin (1991), must "build on (even affirm the value of) current decentralized approaches to academic decision-making" rather than "succumbing to the temptation to centralize control" (p. 248). Bare (1986) advises that the task is to "develop organizational processes that improve performance of the unique academic task. [These processes] must be consistent with existing departmental processes that have evolved over time to grapple with academic problems. Bureaucratic top-down change conflicts fundamentally with these processes" (p. 137).

But injunctions against top-down administration do not mean that central administration has no role in department change. It has a strong role.

The Role of Central Administration in Facilitating Departmental Change

Because each institution differs, readers must adjust these guidelines to their own situation.

Build on departmental autonomy, supporting departmental change initiatives

A study of 21 Michigan State University faculty who were funded to apply new technology and pedagogy to their teaching demonstrates the importance of departmental and central administrative support and resources offered at appropriate times in the innovation process (Davis, Strand, Alexander, and Hussain, 1982). The president of a large public research university known to us spent nearly two years going around to each of the 70-odd departments, listening to what they were doing. At the end, he had a full agenda for change, generated from what was already happening. He began to feature and publicize departments as exemplars and to raise money for their initiatives.

Establish trust, collaboration, clear signals, and shared mission

Blandy and others (1985) emphasize that organizations in which individual units are highly autonomous need high levels of trust between the unit and the central administration and a high level of consensus concerning mission. Some studies link high morale in colleges and universities to the existence of clear institutional missions and goals (Astin, 1987; Cannon and Lonsdale, 1987; Clark, 1970; Gilley, Fulmer, and Reithlingshoefer, 1986; Groner, 1978). Diamond (1993, 1999) suggests how university missions can be used collaboratively to generate department-level missions and goals.

Easterby-Smith (1987) notes that the most top-down, rigidly logical kind of strategic planning entered the academy from the military and was popularized by consultants. A more systemic and cultural version would incorporate descriptive elements, asking how strategies develop in departments. For example, Conrad and Haworth (1992–93) found that decisions about implementing master's programs were not made by a straight goal-then-implementation strategy. Rather, decision makers focused on the particular decision at hand and made choices based on specific areas for consideration, such as their approach to teaching and learning or the amount of support they thought the institution would provide.

Birnbaum (1988) characterizes the role of goals in this way: The president and chief officers select vague goals such as "excellence" and "access" that may be in conflict but that allow flexibility of interpretation at the lower levels of the university (such as departments). Administrators establish certain limited variables, such as graduation rate or the health of the honors program, as indicators that these goals are being met. As problems are brought to their attention, senior administrators consider them sequentially, not in an integrated fashion, without trying to understand the effect of the solution on other units or on the achievement of the overarching goals (pp. 190–191). In such an institution, task forces and planning commissions may produce goal statements, but the functioning of the institution subverts the idealist's picture of planned, sequential, integrated implementation. Pike (2000) proposes that mission and goals *must* differentiate at local levels so as to give local control and allow units such as departments to focus on what they do and care about. These characterizations highlight the administration's highly complex role in mediating, guiding, and influencing goal formation in the department in ways that are not necessarily linear.

A department with considerable autonomy and bad information is a danger to itself and others.

Help the department gather and interpret information

A department with considerable autonomy and bad information is a danger to itself and others. The nature of the information the department has at its command and who gathers, controls, and uses that information are all critical to change, given departmental autonomy. Theus and Billingsley's model for organizational change is especially valuable, we believe, for its emphasis on the role of information: Changes, they say, "all occur as a result of fluctuations or turbulence in environmental conditions, moderated by the amount of information about the environment available to organizational members" (1992, p. 15). Birnbaum (1988) describes the kinds of information needed by the "cybernetic" organization (the organizational model that describes higher education, combining the essential traits of the collegial, bureaucratic, political, and anarchical frames). In such an organization, many points of contact with the outside world must monitor environmental factors, and systems must ensure appropriate dissemination of that information (pp. 196–219). Because in a college or university change cannot be ordered by central administration, says Seymour (1988), institutional research is an important avenue for an institution to become convinced of the need to change (p. 10). Simpson and Sperber (1984), writing to institutional researchers, have commented on departments' lack of information and the lack of departmental staff for gathering and interpreting information. Cost analysis, they note, has been confined to the institution or the state, not the department.

Control of information gives the central administration the power to create a crisis the department did not even know existed. At one large public research university known to us, for example, the provost compiled a list of departments that, according to central administration's statistics, had a high cost per student ratio and were required to improve their ratios or face loss of faculty positions and other resources. The departments themselves had not collected and analyzed the data in those ways, and the whole enterprise of calculating their cost ratio was new to their thinking. They had not envisioned themselves in crisis. They quarreled with the definitions and the interpretation of the data, but in the end, many of them had to make changes. But they remained convinced that they had been unjustly treated.

A different method is to put the information in the department's hands and ask it to conduct the analysis and to benefit from appropriate actions. At one university known to us, comparative departmental productivity data are generated by institutional research through a consortium of institutions (Middaugh, 1995–96, www.udel.edu/ir/cost/). These data are displayed on a Web page accessible to the department. For the department's program review, the provost's guidelines ask the department to analyze the productivity data and state its conclusions. The university gathers comparative data that departments never could but puts the data and the interpretation into departmental hands. The program review at this institution functions as an occasion for administrative control but also for departmental self-analysis (see Wergin, 1999). Another example is the PIRT project, which developed a self-study questionnaire for all its 58 departments to use in understanding their own cultures.

Departments need information not only about costs but also about alternatives (Levin, 1991). For example, one small liberal arts college sends 10 of its faculty each year, as a team, with the provost to a national assessment conference. At the conference, the team spreads out to gather information from the session, then meets at regular intervals for sharing and planning. Attendance by the provost sends a powerful message about the importance of information gathering and planning. Internal communication is important, so that departments know what the others are doing. One of the most powerful aspects of the PIRT project at the University of Cincinnati was that departmental representatives met monthly to share what they were doing to enhance teaching and learning.

Use fiscal incentives tied to goals for change

The budget, says Colton, is "central to the department's operations—and the most important limit on its autonomy" (1995, p. 319; see also Becher and Kogan, 1992; Epstein, 1974; Hackman, 1985; Massy, 1996, p. 14; Rutherford, Fleming, and Mathias, 1985; Salancik and Pfeffer, 1974). At one large research university, the power of the administration to set conditions for resources was revealed when a college dean made an unusual appearance at a department meeting that two of us were observing. He proposed that the department begin a major new initiative in the surrounding community, emphasizing that he was not forcing them to undertake the project. But "I feed the horses that run in my direction," he said, and you could have heard a wisp of hay drop in the room. When he left the department meeting, the members spent the rest of the time discussing not whether but how they would do what he had asked. Zemsky (1995a) drew knowing laughter from an audience at the American Association for Higher Education Faculty Roles and Rewards conference when he said, "There's not a dean worth his or her salt that doesn't know how to put a department in the deep freeze" (see also Zemsky, 1996, p. 1).

One type of reform effort seeks to make more direct and clear the connection between departmental resources and the desired departmental actions. For example, to motivate departments to pay more attention to teaching, a number of institutions have begun to offer awards and resources to departments that demonstrate outstanding teaching or student learning (Kahn, 1996) or to link the departmental budget to a reform agenda such as teaching excellence (Reiser, 1995).

Another way to construct a more direct relationship between student tuition and departmental resources is responsibility-centered management (RCM), being used at the Universities of Michigan, Southern California, and Indiana, among others. RCM remits to the department amounts directly proportional to the tuition they generate and then also charges them for the costs of offering that instruction—for example, faculty salaries, supplies, and sometimes even heat and light. Departments are allowed to carry forward their savings (Massy, 1996; *Change,* September/October 1997, is devoted to RCM). Theoretically, the more tuition a department generates at the least cost, the more discretionary money it has. This system tries to use for teaching the kinds of fiscal awards that have long been used to encourage departments to attract grants and patents: If the department generates the income, it gets to keep part of it.

Administrators have another kind of fiscal power: They can offer resources directly to faculty, bypassing the college and the department. For example, in the mid-1990s at one large research university known to us, $300,000 a year in new money was earmarked for faculty development grants, given directly to faculty applicants by a committee chaired by the university president. The power of this project to remove control from departments and colleges was measured by the complaints of many of the deans and department heads, who argued that the infused funds disrupted their own priorities for building their units. This strategy may not have been a wise way to build "learning" departments, but it demonstrated the power of the central administration to bypass departments' and deans' plans and reward systems.

Not only fiscal resources but student enrollments are in part controlled by the university through its power to establish general education curricula and thus to affect a department's flow of students, majors, and faculty positions (Colton, 1995). Finally, central administration often controls the apportionment of faculty positions—a key resource for departments (Colton, 1995).

Fiscal power, in short, is arguably the central administration's most powerful tool; it can be used effectively to promote change, provided it is exercised with respect for a "learning" department.

Manage crises and deadlines

Hardy, Langley, Mintzberg, and Rose (1984) note crisis as one of the strategies by which the university influences the department (pp. 197–199). To sit in the department meetings of a number of disciplines, as we have done for our PIRT study, is to be reminded how much of a department's energy, timing, resources, and discussion are shaped by what is due (an assessment plan, an annual review, next semester's class schedule, a tenure recommendation) and by what the department thinks is a crisis. In a setting where departmental meeting time is too small to deal with all issues, crises and due dates may co-opt important change efforts, but they may also focus attention or speed the pace of collegial deliberation.

Those who would manage or change departments would do well to explore how resources and energy are structured by the crises and due dates. Ask whether changes in deadlines, in the manner in which deadlines are set, in the issues for which deadlines are established, or in the department's definition of crisis might trigger change in a department's thinking, its priorities, and its allocation of time and resources.

Select and work with department leaders

One avenue for change is for central administration to try to exert greater influence on the selection of chairs. Another is to provide training for chairs. For example, in 1999, the Kansas Regents universities created a committee to develop coordinated training activities for department chairs at its seven institutions. Our study of departments at the University of Cincinnati has impressed us with the extent to which the department chair exercises his or her power in part by appearing, in the eyes of the department, to influence central administration, to garner resources for the department, and to possess accurate information about central administration's actions and intentions. Like a member of Congress, the department chair needs inside information, an occasional dam or army base, and a photo op with the president. We suggest careful examination of the ways in which the administration supports, collaborates with, and exerts influence on chairs.

Like a member of Congress, the department chair needs inside information, an occasional dam or army base, and a photo op with the president.

Create alternative structures

Central administration has power to influence the creation of entities such as institutes, offices of first-year studies, or collaborations with industry that can fulfill some of the department's traditional functions and also do things departments cannot do. David (1997), Zemsky and Massy (1995), and Clark (2000) all suggest that, as such a process expands, the department may become just one of a number of entities within the university competing with other entities for some of the functions for which it once assumed a monopoly. We suggest asking whether such creations would provide welcome relief for a department that cannot perform the whole range of its functions or a threat that galvanizes a department into action. Both administrators and departments need to consider long-term as well as short-term consequences.

Construct forums and processes for university governance

It is easy to view the university in the political frame, with departments and central administration each struggling for power and control (Baldridge, 1971; Baldridge, Curtis, Ecker, and Riley, 1991; Bergquist, 1992; Birnbaum, 1988). But Conrad (1978) long ago urged an extension and correction of the political view by defining the complex types of relationships between the central administration and the departments, especially the role of the administration in brokering decisions and change. Benjamin and Carroll (1998) argue that, instead of an organization in which departments fight for their own advantage and administrators try to balance departmental needs with the needs of others, the university needs a flatter structure in which administrators and departments collaborate for common ends. These structures help department chairs and other leaders transcend mere departmental self-interest and achieve a wider view of the university's and college's situation.

A variety of structural forms has been proposed for such lateral collaboration. One such structure is a first-year program, graduate school dean, or similar office that facilitates coordination among departments (Brown, 1982) and relieves them of some of their work.

A second structural form is the broadly representative decision-making group that brings together central administrators, department heads, students, or representatives of different departments for integrated decision making (Keller, 1989; Tierney, 1999). White (1990) suggests that the university be viewed as a matrix in which departments and faculty are not only in horizontal relations but also in vertical ones, and that faculty should belong simultaneously to a department and to a variety of ad hoc task forces that cross boundaries (see also Perrow, 1986). Clark (2000) suggests a "steering core" of interdisciplinary groups that work to extend the university's entrepreneurial reach. Brown (1982) suggests that proposals for the reform of undergraduate education often seek to form department-like bodies that "reconstitute collegia and extend them to students to permit intellectually meaningful groups of faculty and students to develop curricula and programs" (p. 44). An example in Brown's era was the university college; today it is the learning community.

The past yields cautionary tales about such bodies, however. Levine (1980) describes how, 30 years ago at Buffalo, multidisciplinary undergraduate colleges organized around themes and issues created significant conflict for faculty between allegiance to their own disciplinary departments and the new colleges, to which they supposedly simultaneously belonged. Katz (1987) describes the creation and the mixed success of a widely representative university governance body formed in Ontario in the 1960s (pp. 174–176).

In sum, the injunction against top-down forced change makes great sense, given all the forces that support departmental autonomy. But the dichotomy of top down and bottom up is too simple. The administration has a strong role to play in department change and may sometimes take strong action to influence the department. But such actions, we suggest, must help to form a "learning" department that accurately reads it environment, minimizes defensiveness, and collaborates effectively with the administration to create needed change.

Administrative Roles: A Case History
The importance as well as the difficulties of these roles is illustrated by the University of Cincinnati's Project to Improve and Reward Teaching (for a similar analysis of central administrative leadership in a Southeast Missouri State University general education reform, see Janzow, Hinni, and Johnson, 1996, pp. 508–509). The idea for PIRT

was first proposed by the director of a faculty-development center (coauthor Walvoord) whom the administration had hired as a response to a faculty initiative, and for whom it provided travel funds to the conference where she conceived the idea for PIRT. The central administration supported faculty initiatives and provided the avenues by which new ideas entered the university.

The provost provided visibility and signals by sponsoring and attending informational meetings about PIRT and by providing funds after the initial small grant. Later, when PIRT held an annual two-day retreat a hundred miles away, the president, provost, and several deans drove down each year to participate. One year, the president kept driving, despite tornado warnings in the area (we assume no responsibility if you implement this strategy).

Though funded by the provost, PIRT did not tell departments that they had to join, nor did it tell them how to improve teaching and learning. Departments were asked to conduct a careful self-study and to fashion their own plans. The PIRT office provided a questionnaire and consulting help for the self-study, as well as information, fiscal support, and models of good practice. It also arranged monthly meetings for representatives of all member departments so that departments could collaborate to help one another. It sponsored workshops on topics that departments themselves requested. The self-study and the interdepartmental collaboration enhanced the information that departments had at their command.

In one department, PIRT proponents could make little progress because of some highly dysfunctional departmental dynamics. An associate provost who had expertise in organizational communication initiated a series of workshops for department heads and also acted as a consultant with several departments, including the dysfunctional PIRT member. In another PIRT department, when the self-study uncovered more explosive student dissatisfaction than department members had expected, the college dean paid for consultants to work intensively with both the department and the students. In all these ways, central administrators tried to help departments develop healthy ways of functioning, decision making, and learning.

Meanwhile, the central administration was also supporting other initiatives to improve teaching and student learning:

workshops to help faculty adopt new pedagogies; a revision of general education that would emphasize interactive pedagogies as well as written, visual, and oral communication; faculty development of instructional technology; and compliance with regional accreditors' requirements for assessment of student learning. Thus, from several quarters, departments were perceiving environmental influences that urged more attention to teaching and student learning.

There were two important constraints to achieving PIRT's objectives of enhanced teaching and student learning, however. One constraint was that, while central administration pointed to its support for PIRT as evidence of its support for teaching, departments noted that the promotion and tenure system still emphasized research, that the university allowed departments to become wealthy from grants and patents but not from excellent teaching, and so on. Further, departments were afraid that values and signals might shift with the next dean or provost. Faculty remembered that another program to help departments, formed in the early 1970s, had been closed down. The central administration's challenge is that sending clear and unambiguous signals across the board and across time is very difficult but also very important.

Sending clear and unambiguous signals across the board and across time is very difficult but also very important.

A second constraint on PIRT's achievement of its objectives for teaching and student learning was that teaching was only one of the many tasks the departments had to do. PIRT did not go far enough to address the real and more basic need at the University of Cincinnati and, we would argue, across the nation: to help the department balance all its missions, integrate the various environmental pressures, discern how much time and resources to expend on each initiative, and build healthy ways of decision making and learning.

One avenue for reform, we would suggest, would be a consulting service for departments to help them with those broader issues. In the 1990s, consulting for departments was constructed piecemeal at Cincinnati, aimed primarily at troubled departments. We are talking about a much broader initiative, national in its scope, that would offer consultations to all departments, not just those in deep trouble, helping them to read their environment, discern their own and their institution's best interests, make healthy changes, and learn from their outcomes. Such a service would have to work simultaneously with an institution's central administration as well. The concluding section of this volume develops more fully the total range of functions we envision for such a national center, including research, a clearinghouse, and leadership training, as well as consultation to departments.

Questions for Practitioners

- How do departments in *our* institution exert autonomy and power, and how do deans and central administrators influence them? What avenues for change do these relations suggest?
- How do departmental change initiatives get supported? Could this process be made more fruitful?
- How much do people want clear mission, goals, and signals from deans and central administration? Why do they want them? What channels in this university or college transmit such signals to department members? What form do such signals take? What actions are necessary to validate the message in department members' eyes? Is the culture of the organization open to a rigidly goal-driven planning process? At what level may goals best be formulated, what should they focus on, and how can the goals be owned by the people who are being asked to work toward them? How will progress be measured? What will be the outcome of such measurement?
- How does this department gather and interpret information? Can the administration facilitate that process?
- What are departments' fiscal incentives? Are those incentives consonant with goals for change?
- What crises and deadlines do departments face? How do they apportion their effort around these events? Could the structure be changed?
- How are department leaders selected and supported? Could a different sort of selection or support make possible new initiatives for change?
- What are the structures and processes that enable departments and administrators to work together for the common good? Can they be strengthened? Can new structures be implemented?

DEPARTMENTAL ORGANIZATION, DECISION MAKING, AND INTERACTION

During the 1990s, when the departments in the University of Cincinnati's PIRT set out to construct and implement department-level plans for enhancing undergraduate teaching and learning, they did so in very different ways. Several small departments held a series of meetings with all their faculty, including part-timers, and together arrived at collegial consensus about what was to be done. In other departments, the issue was handed to one of the standing committees, whose recommendations were then brought to the department for comment and approval. In the College of Engineering, where all four departments joined PIRT as a unit, the dean and associate dean selected a committee of representative faculty who, under the guidance of an outside consultant, constructed the plan, which was then implemented with strong direction from the associate dean. In both the latter instances, part-timers were omitted from decision making.

This section explores the various ways in which departments may be organized, how they make decisions, how their members interact, and how those modes may influence change. It describes several possible coexisting frames. Practitioners must analyze their own situation to discover which frames are relevant.

Multiple Frames for Viewing the Department
Departments as collegial
Collegial models for institutions of higher education have often been described (Bergquist, 1992; Birnbaum, 1988; Smart and St. John, 1996; Smart, Kuh, and Tierney, 1997). For departments, based on interviews with 360 faculty from 15 institutions of different types, Massy, Wilger, and Colbeck note that "authentically collegial" departments "emphasize consensus, shared power, consultation, and collective responsibility. . . . Status differences are deemphasized and individuals interact as equals. Members of collegial organizations share aspirations and commitments, have frequent face-to-face interaction, and use civil discourse" (1994, p. 18; see also Wilger and Massy, 1993; Pew Higher Education Roundtable, 1996). Massy, Wilger, and Colbeck found very few authentically collegial departments in their study.

Departments as oligarchic, feudal, or caste-based
When collegial and clan cultures, with their emphasis on consensus decision making among a group of equals, are

not possible or attractive, the system may move toward some mode in which the few govern the many, with different implications for change.

Anderson (1976) describes the department as oligarchic—that is, the rule of the many by the few, who serve their own interests (Robertson, 1993). Although the studies are old, several have suggested that senior professors dominate department meetings and committees, while junior professors have little influence (Ryan, 1972; Williams, 1956). Even when junior faculty are involved in decision making, they may have little real power because what an assistant professor does in a governance role can affect his or her chances for tenure (Hobbs and Anderson, 1971). Ryan (1972) found that smaller departments were more likely to be oligarchic, while larger departments had more committees and involved the faculty more in selecting members.

Crothers (1991) uses the terms "feudal" and "caste-based" to describe departments. He includes a broad group of department "members": (a) faculty, including those who are part time; (b) support staff (secretary, laboratory and computer staff, etc.); (c) research staff (visitors, postdoctoral fellows, etc.); (d) graduate students; and (e) undergraduate students (p. 334). Each group exercises very different levels of power. "Egalitarianism is trumpeted," but the organization is actually "feudal" (p. 342) and "a counter-ideology . . . draws a strong caste line" (p. 335). In relationships among the five "castes" in the department, competition rather than exploitation or violence is the norm, he says, for three reasons: (a) there is sufficient common ground; (b) the prizes cannot be carved up and appropriated privately; and (c) the interests of any one group usually are not gained directly at the expense of others. The prizes for which the groups compete are control of resources and power, but, even more, says Crothers, the prize is respect.

The importance of respect is supported by Groner's study of task structure in 26 Washington state community college divisions and of the departments of a large midwestern university. Departmental task structures that increased "appreciation and understanding of colleagues' work" correlated with a positive group atmosphere in the department (Groner, 1978, p. 141). Yet 20 years later in a survey of 33,986 faculty at 384 colleges and universities, only 32% of them reported that "faculty here respect each other" (University of California at Los Angeles Higher Education Research Institute, 1997). If respect is the prize, few appear to be achieving it. Thomas and Simpson (1995) maintain that collegiality, community, and diversity are not necessarily opposed, though they have seemed to be, because "we in the United States have historically viewed differentness as a means of negating one another's self-worth" (p. 4). Is the loss of respect an inevitable outcome of the department in which different workers perform different tasks and in which members represent a variety of academic backgrounds, interests, ethnic groups, and genders? Can new forms of collegiality overcome these difficulties?

Though Crothers believes that exploitation is rare, the issue has become sharper in the United States recently as both part-time faculty and TAs have made stronger efforts to unionize. Aronowitz (1997) links faculty and TA unionism to movements for social justice, such as civil rights, women's rights, and Vietnam War protests. The TAs represented in Nelson's edited volume (1997) see faculty as members of the elite, protecting their status and condoning if not actively perpetrating the exploitation. Exploitation is the end product of a diverse society that does not operate on mutual respect and protection for the rights of all.

Collegiality exerts a powerful force among academics and is thus potentially a powerful force for change or for resistance to change.

The frames of oligarchy, feudalism, and caste-based systems highlight the heretofore invisible, and now increasingly numerous, department members, including minorities and women, who have perhaps always been left out of the collegium or whose new arrival in departments stretches the boundaries of the traditional collegium beyond what it can easily encompass.

Departments as mixed models

Departments may be predominantly one model or another, but one strand in the literature points to the existence of mixed models. Toombs and Escala call the department "a remarkable concentration of resources, control, and administrative convenience . . . that effectively couples bureaucratic and collegial features" (1987, p. 11). Bolman and Deal (1991) posit that groups may require different forms of structure for different tasks or phases of a task (pp. 115–116). For example, curricular decisions may be made in the collegial mode, while tenure decisions are made by the oligarchy.

Implications for Change
Work within collegial frames

Collegiality exerts a powerful force among academics and is thus potentially a powerful force for change or for resistance to change. It is one of the five core values discussed earlier. Collegiality is one of the chief sources faculty cite for their satisfaction with faculty life, along with workload and autonomy (Pollicino, 1996). The lack of collegiality is one of the reasons faculty cite for leaving professorial life (Olsen, 1992). "Be a good colleague" was marked as an essential or very important professional goal by 86.6% of faculty respondents to a 1995–96 survey of 33,986 faculty from 384 colleges and universities, and there was little variation among types of institutions (University of California at Los Angeles Higher Education Research Institute, 1997). Based on a literature review and on their own interviews with 532 administrators, department chairs, and faculty at 38 campuses that were reasonably representative of American higher education, Bowen and Schuster found that "faculty participation in the making of institutional policies and decisions . . . has a strong influence on faculty morale" (1986, p. 22).

Further, evidence is emerging that institutions of higher education with "clan" cultures are more effective than institutions with other cultures (Dill, 1992, p. 54; Smart and St. John, 1996; Smart, Kuh, and Tierney, 1997). Such cultures exhibit important commonalities with "collegial" cultures described by others. Motivation and supervision are indirect. The most powerful rewards are intrinsic, and extrinsic rewards will have the greatest impact if they can be shared fairly equally. Interaction among members emphasizes collaboration and consensus decision making. Members interact as equals, minimizing status differences. Everyone has a chance to speak and to consider carefully the views of colleagues. Power is wielded through informal networks of influence. Effectiveness is measured, in these studies, by evidence of educational satisfaction among students; students' academic, career, and personal development; faculty members' and administrators' satisfaction with their employment; professional development and quality of the faculty; openness of the system and community interaction; ability to acquire resources; and organizational health (the extent of smooth functioning of the institution in terms of its processes and operations). The question is whether effectiveness would also be linked to collegiality in departments.

Case studies suggest it would. Collegiality is a strong theme in Tobias's case studies of science departments (1992) that are exceptionally successful in educating undergraduates (see especially pp. 39, 158–159). A case study by Parelius and Berlin (1984) concludes that one history department managed decline in enrollments and resources much more effectively than a contrasting history department, in part because of its collegial interaction. Studies of how an economics department adopted a university-wide curriculum review project (V. Smith and others, 1992) and how a health sciences department adopted assessment of student learning (Smith, Scholten, Russell, and McCormack, 1997) emphasize the faculty collegiality that made the changes possible.

Address limitations of collegial systems
Collegial systems in their pure form, however, have several characteristics that may be liabilities, given the external pressures for change we have described.

Time and consensus. One characteristic of collegial systems is their inability to respond quickly, because many people must be consulted and everyone must have time to express his or her point of view. The informal, quasi-political dynamics that operate within collegial systems also require time as people form and shift alliances, gather supporters, and visit colleagues' offices. Those working for change within collegial systems need to allow plenty of time.

That said, our observations in the PIRT study indicate that collegial departments have mechanisms to speed decision making and to avoid having to achieve consensus on every decision. Further research on these mechanisms would be highly valuable. One mechanism that we have observed is representative democracy—a traditional American way of moving beyond the town meeting style of decision making. In departments, this approach means delegating decision making to a committee, an area subgroup, or an individual who takes responsibility for a particular issue (for example, the director of graduate studies or a faculty member who is always willing to work for community-based learning). As noted in the previous section, crises and deadlines may spur such delegation. Several authors have noted the ubiquity and importance of the committee in departments (see, e.g., Colton, 1995; Loftis, 1995). Tucker (1993) and Ryan (1972) began to explore the various types and functions of committees, but further empirical exploration of the varying roles that committees, subgroups, and individuals may play in a department are sorely needed.

Each department appears to have rules about which kinds of decisions need consultation and which do not, which people or committees can be trusted with decisions, and which ones need stronger oversight by the department as a whole or by watchdog members. One strategy for change is to identify and work with those people in the department who enjoy the greatest level of trust from members and who are therefore allowed the greatest freedom to implement change and the greatest credibility in arguing for change.

Timing and the extent of consultation are complex issues in a collegium. A great deal of thought and planning often goes into deciding whether, when, and in what format a decision made by an individual, committee, or chair should be brought back to the entire group for change or ratification. To do so unnecessarily may open the decision to delay or to veto by a small group. But not to bring the decision back to the group may violate their sense of due process. Skillful management of the process can facilitate action.

Another dynamic we have observed in departments is that not all faculty choose to take a strong role in governance. The self-chosen abnegation of some members and the focused participation of others create a department that in fact is run by a smaller group. The possibility that the absent ones will exercise their rights keeps the small group from serving only its own interests.

The implication for change agents is to explore whether such speedier mechanisms can be positive avenues to change without sacrificing the widespread consensus, commitment, and participation that are the strength of collegial systems. Training for chairs and faculty in how to implement such mechanisms is a possible approach to helping departments change.

Evaluation and differential rewards based on outcomes. Another drawback to change is the difficulty that collegial systems experience in evaluating outcomes and assigning differential rewards to their members based on those outcomes. Brown (1982) maintains that formal evaluation and accountability are alien to academic values of autonomy and collegiality (p. 23; see also Mohrman, 1989).

Yet departments do give differential rewards in terms of tenure, and disciplines award differential status for research. A change agent might search for aspects of the department's life where differential rewards are operating in a healthy manner, observe how those rewards work, and build on them. Wergin (1994) suggests another mode: Try to capitalize on the pride that people will feel when the *unit* gets rewarded.

Inward versus outward orientation. Studies of institutions by Smart and his colleagues indicate, as we have said, that "clan" correlates more strongly than other cultures with institutional effectiveness. They have also found, however, that the "adhocracy" culture has some key strengths that are increasingly important for change in the current environment (Smart and St. John, 1996; Smart, Kuh, and Tierney, 1997). Adhocracies emphasize external positioning, a long-term time frame, and achievement-oriented activities. Growth and the acquisition of new resources constitute the primary strategic emphases (Smart and St. John, 1996). The researchers conclude that clan cultures are most successful overall but that adhocracy cultures are strong in student academic development and satisfaction, system openness, and community interaction. These areas are closely related to the ones mentioned in the first two sections of this volume in which contemporary critics demand departmental change—educate students more effectively, collaborate openly among disciplines, respond to competition and to technological advances, and apply knowledge to workplace and community problems. Perhaps current pressures for change focus on precisely those areas where collegial forms are least effective.

Perhaps current pressures for change focus on precisely those areas where collegial forms are least effective.

Explore new models

As noted in the first section of this volume, one group of reform proposals focuses on restoring collegiality, perhaps in somewhat different forms or under new names, and on incorporating new elements such as continuous "quality" or "adhocracy," which stress attending to customers, gathering information about outcomes, monitoring effectiveness, and rewarding individual achievement (Massy, Wilger, and

Colbeck, 1994; Smart and St. John, 1996; see also Birnbaum, 1988, for a description of the "cybernetic" university). Francis and Hampton (1999) present data to argue that research universities as a whole are becoming more market-oriented. Clark (2000) advises departments to adopt "collegial entrepreneurialism." Wergin (1994) recommends that the department adopt aspects of the team, which holds itself collaboratively responsible for outcomes. Likewise, the literature on the "learning organization" emphasizes aspects of collegiality but adds two new elements: (a) articulating underlying values and assumptions, which may remain unexpressed or be taken for granted in old-style collegiality; and (b) evaluating the effects of the group's decisions so that group learning can take place.

Wergin (1994) reports the results of his nationwide search for departments that were truly collaborative as teams and institutions whose policies supported and rewarded such behavior. He found none so instead presented case studies of institutions that had made a start down the road. Massy, Wilger, and Colbeck (1994) found very few "authentically" collegial departments, let alone any that integrated quality principles. Rutherford, Fleming, and Mathias (1985) fail to provide living examples of departments that follow the learning organization or what they term the "model 2" practices. There may be a lesson here. Why do such departments not exist? Is it that there are some basic departmental needs or functions not served by authentic collegiality, teams, or learning organizations?

Clearly, higher education is still searching for new forms of organization and decision making that actually can and do exist in academic departments. Perhaps in addition to importing concepts from business such as "team" and "learning organization," higher education needs research to identify how departments are inventing new forms. Practitioners need to experiment with new forms in their own settings. The last section of this volume suggests a national initiative to conduct the needed research, identify best practices, and help departments change.

A Case Study

An example of how one department interacted in a collegial way yet also faced conflict and implemented assessment is reported by Smith, Scholten, Russell, and McCormack (1997) in an Australian university. (In the article, the word "staff" refers to faculty, following the British terminology.) In a health sciences department, supported by newly available funds for assessment and spurred by students' complaints, a small group of the members, who had been taking a course on teaching, led an initiative to hold five workshops to help faculty assess student learning in the undergraduate degree program. The workshops, facilitated by an external coordinator, were sufficiently successful that the department then decided to institutionalize four meetings per year to continue the assessment process—a mark of success in institutionalizing change. Several principles emerged that, according to the authors, account for the success of the project: (a) the outside facilitator was very skillful in leaving ownership in the hands of department members; (b) assessment was viewed as a socially constructed event in which members' participation and process were crucial to success; (c) the group transcended "comfortable collaboration," characterized by reluctance to face conflict, and achieved "critical collaboration," in which the group questions its own culture and actions to arrive at a problem-solving agenda, then encourages a shared commitment to explore contradictions and to seek ethical justification. The department, in other words, worked simultaneously to strengthen authentic collegiality, to be more attuned to its students and its external environment, to face conflict head on, and to assess outcomes of its work and use that information to inform the department's ongoing decisions.

Questions for Practitioners

- What do department members think collegiality is? Do all the department members believe their department is collegial? How would they suggest making it more effectively collegial? How can collegial modes lead to change?
- If the slow pace and the need for consensus are a hindrance to change, what mechanisms exist for speeding up the process or for decision making by a smaller group? Can these processes be harnessed for change?
- In what ways, or from whose point of view, is this department oligarchic, feudal, or caste-based? Do these aspects have negative consequences for the department, or do they operate as a positive part of the mix of

governance modes? How can change initiatives arise within these modes?

- How does this department evaluate its environment, outcomes, and strategies? How does it evaluate and reward its members? Would members be open to further evaluation? How could this evaluation be conducted so as to preserve collegiality?

DEPARTMENTAL LEADERSHIP

Leadership is critical for departmental effectiveness and change. Strong leadership has been found to be a crucial factor in the high morale of 10 outstanding colleges (Rice and Austin, 1988). Kozma's study (1985) of Exxon- and National Science Foundation–funded projects for instructional innovation demonstrated that the role of the chair was crucial in achieving the projects' goals. Faculty development leaders (Wright, 1994) and provosts (Edwards, 1999) in surveys strongly agree on the importance of departmental leadership. The Pew Higher Education Roundtable has cited strengthening the role of the chair as one of the four steps needed to help departments meet the challenges of the changing environment (Zemsky, 1996, p. 9). This section is addressed to chairs and to those who work with them, inside and outside the department.

The role of department leaders other than the chair has not been well studied (Bensimon, Neumann, and Birnbaum, 1989); hence, this section focuses mainly on chairs. Senge (1996, 2000), however, points to the importance of local networkers in learning organizations. Our own observations of departments in the PIRT study affirm the importance and influence of faculty members who lead committees, take on projects, act as watchdogs for process, have been chair, will be chair, serve as president of the union, attract grants or good students, or know how to make a computer do what the operator wants.

Characteristics of Chairs
The chair's leadership depends on context
As an alternative to the functionalist perspective, which assumes that managers can manipulate toward desired ends, recent theorists have emphasized that peoples' values, perceptions, personal qualities, symbols and myths, and models of leadership all help to construct what they think a good leader is and how they influence, interpret, and respond to the actions of the leaders (Bensimon and Neumann, 1993; Neumann and Larson, 1997; Deetz, 1992; Dill, 1984; Lueddeke, 1999). Dill (1984) notes that "academic management is an ambiguous process highly dependent on flows of influence and power, and subject to the beliefs and values of the academic culture" (p. 92). Mitchell's study (1987) of 19 outstanding chairs at three universities in the Midwest found that effective leadership depended on the congruent

interaction among leaders' values and management strategies, values of the faculty and administration, control over resources, and the department's stage of development. Thus, in times of change, departmental notions of leadership may themselves be changing and may affect change. Practitioners must analyze their own situation, using this section in suggestive, not prescriptive, ways.

Neumann and Larson (1997) articulate the challenge facing department chairs, noting that leaders must integrate responses to external realities with consideration of faculty values—especially difficult in eras where those two elements may be in conflict. They recommend a leadership style that inverts normal hierarchy, with leadership emerging from below as well as from above. Department chairs are the "below" in some settings, the "above" in others. They are positioned, then, at the crossroads of institutional planning and change.

Chairs have multiple allegiances and multiple tasks

Many chairs view themselves primarily as faculty serving a relatively short term, with the average six years (Carroll, 1991; Seagren, Wheeler, Creswell, Miller, and Van Horn–Grassmeyer, 1994). Bennett (1982) identifies three entities that compete for the chair's allegiance: the department, the institution, and the discipline. The chair does not exercise full power or entirely control the rewards in any of these entities.

Chairs' roles and responsibilities have been expanding over the last decade (Lucas, 2000b, p. 10). Seagren, Wheeler, Cresswell, Miller, and Van Horn–Grassmeyer (1994), in a survey of 2,875 community college chairs, found that they worked an average of 31 to 40 hours per week just on their duties as chair. Dill's review of the literature (1984) found that the amount of time spent on duties as a chair is a major source of stress for department heads and deans. Tension occurs among administrative duties, which keep the department functioning smoothly; faculty development activities; and strategic activities such as planning. Seagren, Wheeler, Cresswell, Miller, and Van Horn–Grassmeyer (1994) found that the overwhelming majority of chairs in both community colleges and four-year institutions believed that "very important" tasks included all three—administrative duties, faculty development activities, and strategic activities—though

Carroll and Gmelch (1992) found that chairs focused their efforts differentially on scholarly, faculty development, management, and strategic leadership tasks. Chairs may wield very different powers in different departments, even within the same institution (Lucas, 2000b, p. 11). Administrators may believe that all duties are important (Falk, 1979), or they may believe that chairs' key duties are primarily administrative (Moxley and Olson, 1990).

Chairs wield ambiguous power

Bensimon, Neumann, and Birnbaum (1989) point to the importance of Kerr and Jermier's heretofore neglected theory (1978) that in organizations such as universities and colleges, certain forces (e.g., faculty autonomy and peer-based reward structures) substitute for, or blunt the power of, traditional functions that leaders exercise in hierarchical organizations. Such theories help to explain the limited control that department chairs exercise over budget, rewards, curriculum, and personnel issues.

But chairs do exercise certain types of power. Legitimate power, what Leslie (1973) would call "formal authority," stems from the chair's right to make decisions and to affect procedural issues such as the membership of committees. Chairs also enjoy an ability to frame issues to their advantage. They often have special knowledge and membership on committees and coalitions (Seagren, Creswell, and Wheeler, 1993). They define reality; they conceptualize problems (Deetz, 1992). In a learning department, where information is the basis of genuine deliberation, the power to gather and shape information is critical.

Second, chairs may be able to give rewards, such as merit pay, reappointment, promotion, and tenure. Beyond this power, as Deetz (1992) notes, the chair has power as "the accountant": what counts in workload, how to calculate teaching load, and how much money is in each account. Deetz and others have noted, however, that the chair's responsibilities are disproportionately large in relation to his or her ability to reward faculty behaviors (Edwards, 1999), which leads to the tension between the faculty behaviors the chair must organize and the rewards the chair is able to give.

Third, expert power, or functional authority (Leslie, 1973), may result from personal skills and technical competence.

That power is based on respect, the chair's standing in the discipline and the institution, interpersonal effectiveness, knowledge of how to accomplish things in the university, access to information about administrative plans and decisions, and perceived credibility with administration and faculty (Lucas, 1989). McKeachie (1976) argues that the power of the chair depends in part on his or her stubbornness with superiors, problem-solving skills, and time and energy. Deetz (1992) observes that a chair's direct influence is aided by being multilingual—being able to discuss various subgroups' goals—or being capable of building a coalition between competing subgroups and goals while fulfilling his or her own goals.

We would suggest that an additional type of power is the power of information. Chairs have access to information both above and below them in the hierarchy. If they use this information wisely, they have the power to establish priorities for their effort and to muster resources for change.

Chairs have little formal training for the job

Edwards (1999) lists lack of training as one of the most important and problematic characteristics of department chairs. The issue is perhaps not just the training itself but the implications: the untrained "peer" chair belongs to the collegial culture; training implies more of the managerial culture (Bergquist, 1992).

Implications for Change

What avenues for change arise from consideration of the characteristics of chairs?

Analyze the culture

Because leadership is so dependent on context, it is important for department leaders to study the culture in which they are embedded (Bensimon, Neumann, and Birnbaum, 1989). Ask how the people in the department, as well as the people in the central administration, view the role of the department chair. What do they think good leadership is? What do they think their own roles are? Every further suggestion in this section must be adapted to the local context.

Make time for strategic planning

Given the tension between strategic and administrative duties, change may occur if chairs or other department leaders have more time for strategic planning. Retreats and release time are short-term moves in this direction; provision of extra personnel such as secretaries and assistant heads offer long-term support. Or chairs may simply decide to reapportion their time.

Change the chair's power

An avenue for change is to enhance or decrease the chair's power in any of three areas—legitimate, reward, or expert power. McAdams (1997) and Edwards (1999) especially note that department chairs exert little control over rewards, given their responsibilities for allocating tasks. A Lehigh University task force recommended giving chairs more budgetary autonomy, emphasizing their leadership rather than merely management roles, and giving them more support for development (McAdams, 1997).

Institutionally, the power of the chair may change in other ways. For example, at the University of Cincinnati, the fact that chairs are members of the union exerts a strong influence, both real and symbolic, on the types of power they wield. To change that alignment would cause other changes.

Combine "consideration" with "structure-initiation"

The literature affirms that the keys to successful change are "empathy, communication, and participation" (Lueddeke, 1999, p. 236; see also Dill, 1984). Some studies suggest, however, that leaders need to be both *considerate* (focus on relationships, be friendly, consult with colleagues, communicate with subordinates) and *structure-initiating* or *task-oriented* (direct and clarify work roles, solve problems, criticize poor work). Both consideration and structure-initiation are related to effectiveness (Hemphill, 1955; McCarthy, 1972; Mitchell, 1987) and to high regard by faculty (Knight and Holden, 1985).

The greatest difference that Mitchell (1987) noted among the outstanding department chairs in three urban comprehensive midwestern universities were their beliefs about appropriate management styles: Some advocated a democratic style, but many chose a more autocratic style. "'Previously [according to the chair], all decisions were held up to a vote.' This might work in some situations, but here 'senior faculty were not producing at full potential' and 'the department was not acting as a unit.' Professional freedom and democracy had produced a faculty with 'a lot of promise but not much performance.' Only through strong direction was this chairperson able to turn an average department into a very effective one with excellent research performance and high-quality graduate students" (pp. 168–169). A more democratic style may work better in other situations or for other goals, but the individual situation must dictate the management style.

Guskin and Bassis (1985) propose a taxonomy of chairs based on how they exercise their powers. *The hero* possesses significant power and delegates little; this style reduces entrepreneurial activity, heightens tension with faculty, and does not lead to consensus. *The mediator* emphasizes negotiation and compromise, but the downside is a failure to be innovative, divisions between units, and wasted time. *The team leader* delegates authority and stimulates discussion in an atmosphere of mutual respect to generate creativity and innovation. The authors believe the team leader is the most effective style.

Lucas (2000b) proposes a "team leader" model in which the chair is neither an autocrat nor a peer. She outlines 12 principles for the successful team leader that emphasize (a) shared goals and problem solving, motivation, trust, and participation; (b) monitoring by the team of its own effectiveness against a high standard of excellence; and (c) effective conflict management.

Perhaps most germane to this volume's emphasis on the need for collegial forms combined with more outward- and results-oriented modes is Ramsden's discussion (1998) of the leadership styles implied by the collegial, bureaucratic, corporate, and enterprise cultures. Collegial leadership is a servant leadership, achieved through consensual background activity. Enterprise leadership is entrepreneurial; it functions as guidance, enablement, articulation of vision, and support for achieving tasks (p. 265). The literature suggests that departments must, according to their individual situations, find the right kind of integration of collegial and enterprise leadership.

Develop the chair's skills or leadership style
One resource for chairs is advice books (see, e.g., Bensimon, Ward, and Sanders, 2000; Gmelch and Miskin,

1993; Gillett-Karam, 1999; Hecht, Higgerson, Gmelch, and Tucker, 1999; Lucas, 1994; Lucas and Associates, 2000; Seagren, Cresswell, and Wheeler, 1993; Tucker, 1993). All of these sources must be used in light of our earlier point: Leadership is highly dependent on context.

Training for chairs is a common prescription among reformers, both for helping chairs to develop needed skills and for developing new visions of departmental inter-action and leadership. Though Dill (1984) concludes that seminars and continuing professional development do little good for chairs (p. 89), the visionaries who propose the "learning organization" rely heavily on outside consultants who work with departments to help them change and on leadership teams who undertake intensive training over long periods of time (e.g., Senge, 1996, 2000). A number of training programs for chairs are described in the literature (e.g., Filan, 1999; Foote, 1999). Theories that emphasize the context-dependent nature of leadership and the dispersion of leadership throughout the department suggest not just training for chairs in a retreat setting or one-shot consulting, but an initiative in which a consultant works with the de-partment in its own setting over time; in which department teams, rather than just chairs, attend retreats; in which ad-ministrators and chairs work together to create a context in which departments can function effectively; and in which training focuses on articulating the values, theories in use, and systemic environments in which the department operates.

Questions for Practitioners
- Who are the departmental leaders, both informal and formal? What kinds of power do they or could they wield? Can this power be altered to facilitate change?
- What do department members think a good leader should do?
- What style do leaders use? How do they spend their time? Could change enter through a change in style or redistri-bution of energy and time?

DEPARTMENTAL WORK, FACULTY ROLES, AND REWARDS

Many of the demands for change noted in the first section concern departmental work and faculty roles: improve undergraduate learning, redistribute faculty labor between research and teaching, deliver education more broadly across boundaries of time and space, collaborate across disciplines, apply knowledge to real-world problems, and be more cost-effective. Of all the areas we have addressed, perhaps faculty work, roles, and rewards is the area where change will be the most necessary and the forces for change most far-reaching.

The first point with implications for change is that the department must perform its work but does not entirely control it. Then we examine the various ways in which departments are struggling to accommodate five forces: (a) proliferation of non-tenure-track faculty and faculty who are dispersed in terms of location and/or time of day (currently, about half of all new hires in U.S. colleges and universities are part time and about one-fourth are full time but not tenure track [Schuster, 2000]); (b) the advent of costly technologies that allow teaching to transcend traditional boundaries of time and space; (c) changing patterns of student demographics and expectations; (d) the rise of competing educational providers; and (e) the unbundling of traditionally bundled faculty and departmental tasks. Our thesis in this section is that these forces challenge traditional modes for departmental allocation of tasks, productivity, quality control, hiring, faculty socialization, faculty development, and faculty rewards. Departments are groping toward new modes. This section is closely linked to, and builds upon, our arguments in "Departmental Organization, Decision Making, and Interaction" about the need to find new modes of organization and decision making to establish viable new forms of collegiality and to add new elements such as outward-orientation and evaluation of outcomes.

Multiple Influences Define the Department's Work

In defining its work, the department faces multiple influences. Earlier sections have discussed the ways in which external stakeholders exert pressure and the ways in

Cecilia Lucero, a doctoral candidate in higher education at the University of Michigan and intern in the Kaneb Center for Teaching and Learning at the University of Notre Dame, contributed to this section.

which the discipline and the institution help define and control the department's work. Departmental work is also shaped by the autonomy of faculty and by their inclination to see work as their own individual work, not primarily the department's work, especially if they have tenure and/or if they are highly productive in research (Mohrman, 1989, p. 69). A 1989 survey of 5,400 faculty from all institutional types indicated that many faculty feel greater commitment to the discipline than to the department or the institution (Boyer, 1990). Massy (1996) notes, "In thinking about incentives, one must keep in mind that the issue is faculty time allocation and that, for many faculty, every hour shifted from research risks a significant loss of earnings potential" (p. 14; see also Blackburn, Horowitz, Edington, and Klos, 1986; Brown, 1982, pp. 96, 116–117; Ramey and Dodge, 1983, p. 417).

The concept of "slack" helps explain the sense of entitlement that characterizes faculty members' definitions of their work.

The concept of "slack" is useful in understanding individual faculty members' relations to the department (Manns and March, 1978). If the performance of an organization exceed its goals, it reaps "slack" and can give its members benefits such as comforts, reduced supervision, and lighter workloads. When the organization attempts higher goals, slack may diminish. In the academy, the relation between the department's achievements and the existence of slack may be masked by the complexity and autonomy of faculty work, the department's separation from the tuition that pays its bills, and the difficulty of measuring outcomes of its work. The benefits of slack, such as a certain teaching load, may come to be seen as rights. The concept of "slack" helps explain the sense of entitlement that characterizes faculty members' definitions of their work.

Lacking total control of its work, the department must nevertheless meet expectations for that work. It must act to ensure appropriate allocation of tasks, productivity, the quality of its work, the reward systems that support its faculty, and the quality of life for its faculty and its students. The rest of this section discusses the enormous contemporary pressures that make such tasks difficult. Table 1 summarizes how departments are moving in response to these pressures. At the end, we discuss implications for change.

TABLE 1

Changes in Departmental Work, Faculty Roles, and Rewards

	Traditional Collegial Mode (a powerful ideal, but probably never fully realized in practice, even in the Good Old Days)	*Newer Modes*	*Future Modes*
Allocation of tasks	Tasks apportioned informally and flexibly among equal colleagues.	Delegate to non-tenure-track faculty and others with named titles (such as "lecturer" or "adjunct") that define work and status.	Sharing of tasks with industry trainers, computer specialists, etc. Unbundle tasks formerly integrated: e.g., one company does the testing, while another does computer-based instructional design.
Enhancement of productivity	Increase class size within traditional lecture-test mode.	Delegate recitation, paper grading, and lab supervision to adjuncts or TAs. Hire low-paid adjuncts or TAs to teach introductory courses.	Use computer to "capitalize" part of faculty work: e.g., interactive CD-ROMs or DVDs for instruction in introductory courses such as chemistry and calculus. Use distance learning to increase class size beyond limits of physical classroom size.
Quality control	Depends on socialization, shared professional norms, and interaction with colleagues. Tenure decision admits the colleague to membership,	More adjuncts and non-tenure-track faculty means that many teachers cannot interact with colleagues or are not socialized in traditional	Faculty are increasingly diverse and dispersed, geographically and chronologically. New modes of quality control include outcomes

TABLE 1

Changes in Departmental Work, Faculty Roles, and Rewards (*continued*)

	Traditional Collegial Mode (a powerful ideal, but probably never fully realized in practice, even in the Good Old Days)	*Newer Modes*	*Future Modes*
	after which there is no formal review. Judgments of the department's quality are based on input measures such as faculty qualifications, curriculum, and so on.	ways. Thus, old modes of quality control break down or are partly replaced by more bureaucratic modes such as outcomes assessment and annual review of faculty. Assessment is driven by accreditation bodies and legislatures, and focuses on outcomes. Departments do it for compliance.	assessment, on-line collaboration, standardization of syllabi, use of prepackaged instructional elements such as interactive CD-ROMs or DVDs, etc. Assessment of student learning outcomes is the basis of heated competition among alternative providers. Departments do it to survive.
Hiring	Department exercises strong autonomy in hiring. Colleagues hire others much like themselves through old boy networks. Job descriptions focus on disciplinary specialization.	New hires are increasingly diverse. Other stakeholders play a larger role in hiring (e.g., affirmative action, central administration). Adjuncts and lecturers are hired by chair without the significant interaction of colleagues accorded to tenure-track hiring. Job description varies with role: e.g., teaching specialists.	Increasingly diverse and specific job descriptions as tasks disaggregate (e.g., distance education specialist, computer specialist). Increasingly diverse and bureaucratic modes of hiring. Department must work closely with some people it does not hire.

Faculty socialization and development	Conducted by colleague mentoring and interaction. Faculty member has flexibility to informally change his or her mix of tasks at different points in his or her career.	Decline in mentoring and interacting with colleagues as faculty diversifies and becomes more competitive. Formal faculty development workshops and mentoring programs attempt to fill the gap.	Increased on-line collaboration and other modes help to overcome diversification and dispersion of faculty members. Increasing need for lifelong training in computer-based and other specialized aspects.
Faculty rewards	Rewards center on teaching and are largely intrinsic. Rewards equalized among colleagues.	Faculty become more individualistic. Salary gap between stars and regular faculty increases. Multiple rewards available to faculty as research increases.	Increasingly diverse rewards for faculty and increasing disparity of rewards. Those on the bottom (adjuncts, TAs) use methods traditional to the worker underclass: unionization, focus on self-interest and mobility.

How Does the Department Allocate Tasks?

The literature suggests that groups with uncertain and complex tasks employ high levels of horizontal communication and informal coordination (Bare, 1986, p. 133). In the traditional collegium, a group of equal faculty members informally divided the work among themselves by consensus (Bergquist, 1992; Birnbaum, 1988; Massy, Wilger, and Colbeck, 1994; Smart and St. John, 1996; Smart, Kuh, and Tierney, 1997). This ideal was never fully realized and collegial systems have their own flaws; nevertheless, the ideal of collegiality is still a powerful factor in departmental life, and some evidence indicates that the collegial model is the most highly successful governance model for higher education. As faculty increasingly differ in rank, title, status, and pay, and as they are dispersed by location and time of day, however, the modes of apportioning departmental tasks are shifting from collegial agreement among equals toward other modes of delegation.

One mode of delegation is formal task differentiation marked by title. For example, "adjunct," "lecturer," "associate" (Indiana University), and "professor of the practice of" the discipline (Duke) all imply more undergraduate teaching and lower status than tenured faculty (see Bowen and Schuster, 1986; Fulton, 2000; Gappa, 1997).

Another mode is delegation to nonfaculty workers or units. For example, advising may be done in the dean's office or in student affairs. TAs may do grading. Remedial instruction or testing may be delegated to a for-profit agency. Computer-based instruction may require not only faculty but technicians and instructional designers. These developments are part of a larger unbundling of tasks that used to be inevitably linked: curriculum, instruction, advising, mentoring, and testing. For example, one university mathematics department we know hired a for-profit company to conduct remedial math instruction for its students. Western Governor's University grants degrees on the basis of students' demonstrated competence. It employs advisers for students and advisory boards for assessment and competency construction but relies largely on external testing firms to produce and deliver its tests and on other institutions to offer instruction by which its students gain the competencies WGU requires (Young, 1999; www.wgu.edu).

How Does the Department Enhance Productivity?

Productivity in its industrial context means producing the highest possible output with the lowest possible input (Tierney, 1999, pp. 41–42). In research and administration, departmental productivity has been achieved, much as in industry, by increased automation and technology. Productivity in teaching, however, has been achieved by enlarging classes and by delegating some duties to lower-paid people. Reformers, as noted earlier, call for more radical changes, suggesting that computers do some of the presentation of basic information and concepts and some of the drill and response that faculty used to do (Massy and Zemsky, 1995). They suggest that faculty use electronic means to provide instruction across boundaries of space and time. In the future, "students will spend more time learning by themselves and with their peers and much more time engaged with powerful, interactive technologies, and will spend less actual time—but more creative, intensive, and focused time—with faculty members. Faculty, in turn, will work with greater numbers of students but 'teach' much less" (Guskin, 1994, p. 19).

Use of computers to take over former faculty work poses both practical and cultural problems. First, the roles that computers assume—delivery of formerly lectured instruction or facilitation of student peer collaboration—may challenge faculty members' sense of identity as disciplinary specialists—a high value in the academy. Moreover, computers are expensive. At one institution we know, the engineers purchase top-of-the-line computers from their considerable grant/patent income and pass their used computers down to faculty in less wealthy departments. Their generosity is admirable, but the implications for departments are serious indeed, as less wealthy departments scramble to find the resources to keep up.

The roles that computers assume—delivery of formerly lectured instruction or facilitation of student peer collaboration—may challenge faculty members' sense of identity as disciplinary specialists.

How Does the Department Control the Quality of Its Work?

Quality control for non-tenure-track faculty

Collegial methods of quality control are based on the assumption that all colleagues share similar norms and values, gained during graduate school and reinforced by daily interaction. But as faculty increasingly diversify and disperse and as departments collaborate with industry trainers or testing firms, the new workers may not share the same socialization experiences, come up for tenure review by the faculty, or engage in frequent interaction with other departmental faculty. In the worst cases, the departmental work performed by non-tenure-track faculty or by other entities becomes invisible and unsupervised. Perhaps a harried chair tries to interview adjuncts carefully and to keep an eye on what they do, but few resources, scant appreciation, and not much importance are attached to this work. Alternatively, the department may turn to methods such as outcomes assessment.

Assessment of outcomes
The requirement by regional accreditors, boards, and other constituencies that institutions and their departments use assessment of student outcomes for improvement and the attachment of sanctions and resources to outcomes challenge the traditional process-oriented and resource-oriented ways in which departments have typically measured their effectiveness and the traditional assumptions behind the grading process. The evidence suggests that increasing numbers of departments are assessing student learning outcomes, often at the behest of accrediting agencies or boards and legislatures. Views differ on whether assessment has effected meaningful reform (see, e.g., Banta, 1996; Lazerson, Wagener, and Shumanis, 2000), but in the landscape of the future, Armstrong (2000) argues, alternative providers will use data about learning outcomes to demonstrate that they can do as well as or better than traditional institutions in teaching students, and legislators will increasingly base funding on such demonstrations of outcomes. Assessment will become the coin of the realm for survival, not just a nuisance requirement.

How Does the Department Hire Its Faculty?
Differential control over the hiring process
The department exerts strong and jealous control of the hiring process for tenure-track faculty, as is appropriate in an organization that relies heavily on preestablished norms and values in its workers. The department faculty develop the job description (with pro forma help from an affirmative action office), interview candidates, establish the criteria by which candidates will be judged, and make the primary recommendation for hiring.

For adjunct and other non-tenure-track faculty, however, the process is less careful and collegial. In these cases, the search committee often disappears entirely, and the department chair or program director interviews candidates and decides who will be hired. In this way, the hiring process maintains and affirms differential tasks, pay, career tracks, roles, and status. Such hiring also invites problems for a system that depends heavily on the careful hiring of people who exhibit the norms and values of the group and whose membership in the group is the chief mode of quality control.

Focus on disciplinary specialization

The concerns of the discipline tend to be very powerful in the hiring process for tenure-track faculty. The department tends to see its work as the management of areas of knowledge. Thus, the department tends to define its tenure-track positions by the research area to be "covered" by the new faculty member, even if the tenure line itself was granted on the basis of the department's need for full-time faculty coverage of its introductory courses. The person who was hired might teach fewer undergraduate nonmajors than the adjunct she or he was supposedly hired to replace and might envision his or her optimum career track as a gradual reduction in undergraduate teaching (Zemsky, 1993). The adjunct in fact might never be let go but continue to teach as in the past. At some universities, adjunct positions are not separately designated in the department's budget but come from the department's general funds; thus, the department can add or subtract adjunct positions without seeking explicit central administrative authorization.

A provost at a research university calls this whole process "faculty creep." "I authorize a tenure-track position to reduce adjunct coverage of introductory general education courses, and the department hires a full-time person. Then, a couple of years later, I turn around and look again, and there is the same ratio of adjunct coverage for general education courses."

Categorizations for new hires are sometimes embedded in the department's governance system. For example, in English departments we have observed, faculty "area committees" take responsibility for courses in various areas: medieval studies, early American literature, composition, and so on. When a new position is considered, the question is posed, which area will get the new position? Then that particular area committee plays a major role in the search. Within such a structure, hiring a new faculty member who does not fit into one of the already defined areas becomes difficult.

The categorizations and assumptions under which new faculty enter the department help to establish their expectations and behaviors, sometimes far into the future. When the chair in one research department we have observed increased the number of nonmajor, writing-intensive courses that each faculty member was expected to teach, one senior faculty member, hired eight years previously, complained that he had been hired to build the program in medieval studies and should not have to teach writing-intensive seminars to first-year undergraduates.

How Does the Department Socialize and Develop Its Faculty?

Socialization and faculty development are modes by which the department guides and supports the career-long growth of its faculty and assures the quality of their work by inculcating common norms and values.

Formal orientation and faculty development programs

Formal orientation and faculty development programs have arisen to fill the socialization and development needs unmet within increasingly dispersed collegial groups. Rosch and Reich (1996) found, however, that formal orientation and faculty development programs were "an extremely limited portion of the socialization experience" for junior faculty (p. 126). Fink (1992) found that orientation or workshop attendance rates by new faculty vary by the extent to which the department or central administration supports or mandates the activity—an indication that faculty look to their departments and central administrators as the chief source of information and advice about their jobs.

Importance of departmental collegial guidance

Informal departmental collegial guidance is and probably always will be overwhelmingly the dominant mode for socialization and faculty development (Olsen and Sorcinelli, 1992; Tierney 1997). As collegial groups become more dispersed, however, informal departmental socialization may not adequately meet the needs of new faculty. Reynolds's ethnographic study of new faculty on two campuses (1992) found that faculty "bemoaned the lack of substantive interaction with colleagues. . . . [One said] it made me extremely unhappy because this is a place where you could sit in your office for weeks, literally, and no one would ever come by for any reason" (p. 646). After several years of being left to sink or swim, one new faculty member said, "The department was a 'fiefdom system' where there was 'no collegiality' and 'no shared interest.' He found it difficult to talk with his colleagues because of the constant need to speak in a politically acceptable way (p. 642). In the area of teaching, Boice (1991) found that "of all kinds of advice and support [reported by new teachers], counsel about teaching was least often reported" (p. 155). In predominantly white male departments, women and people of color may have fewer opportunities to be mentored by senior faculty (Tierney and Rhoads, 1993, p. 66). Non-tenure-track faculty are often excluded from whatever collegial guidance exists (Fulton, 2000; Gappa and Leslie, 1993).

The lack of early collegial support may have long-lasting effects. Boice (1993) found that the patterns of "collegial isolation/neglect," "collegial disapproval," "self-doubts about competence," and feelings of victimization and suspicion among disillusioned midcareer faculty often had their origins in pretenure incidents (p. 38).

How Does the Department Reward Its Faculty?
Rewards are shaped by culture

The core academic values we mentioned—autonomy, collegiality, rationality, specialization, and academic freedom—as well as the values and cultures of individual institutions, will help to determine what is valued as a reward. When faculty are asked what they like most about their profession, autonomy and collegiality are high on the list (Pollicino, 1996). Hence, autonomy, collegiality, relief from time pressures, or resources to do one's work may themselves function as rewards, and they may affect the meaning of other rewards.

Some kinds of rewards may not be as highly valued as one might expect, especially if they compete with other rewards, compromise academic values, or heighten stress. For example, new faculty at research universities sometimes

New faculty at research universities sometimes have confided to us that they are afraid of winning an award for teaching, lest it be held against them at tenure time.

have confided to us that they are afraid of winning an award for teaching, lest it be held against them at tenure time.

Faculty rewards have multiple sources

Faculty experience the academy as a setting that offers multiple rewards, and they have considerable autonomy to choose among those rewards. No one entity controls all the rewards that faculty or departments can achieve. Consequently, when the central administration creates a departmental reward for teaching or when the department creates a faculty reward for teaching, those rewards do not co-opt the entire reward system; they become additional rewards in a multiple-reward system.

Intrinsic and extrinsic rewards intertwine

Intrinsic rewards are very important to faculty (Froh, Menges, and Walker, 1993). For example, respect of colleagues is so important in academe that Crothers (1991) names it as the prize for which all members of a department strive. In higher education, however, intrinsic and extrinsic rewards are inseparable in practice. Extrinsic rewards often have symbolic and cultural value that give them an intrinsic meaning to the faculty member (Hearn, 1999). For example, a promotion in rank is an extrinsic reward, but it has a symbolic value beyond the money it may bring; it is also a key to some important intrinsic rewards such as the esteem of colleagues and a sense of satisfaction with one's own performance. Intrinsic rewards such as the respect of colleagues may translate into promotion or mobility, which bring extrinsic rewards in salary.

The career ladder is flat

One mechanism by which an organization rewards and guides its members is the career ladder and the criteria and standards that are applied for each successive rung. For tenure-track faculty, the tenure decision and to a lesser extent the promotion to full professor function as powerful focal points of attention and effort. But the faculty career ladder has only a few rungs. For non-tenure-track faculty, it may have no rungs at all, either in promotion or in salary. The department must encourage changes and growth across a faculty member's career without the structure of a multirung career ladder.

Performance criteria and standards are often ambiguous

Faculty work is so complex that it is difficult to establish explicit guidelines or to measure adherence. Gmelch, Wilke, and Lovrich's 2,000-subject study in 1986 pointed out that "the general absence of clear and standardized guidelines for judging faculty performance causes a good deal of faculty stress with respect to pay, promotion and career advancement" (1986, p. 267). Inadequate feedback and reward is one of the primary sources of stress for junior faculty (Lamber and others, 1993, p. 23).

Competitive rewards may counter collegial traditions

Although some argue that evaluation of faculty by one another violates the basic egalitarian spirit of collegiality (e.g., Brown, 1982; Hirst and Blomquist, 1994), department members have long made evaluative judgments of one another in hiring, tenuring, and promoting tenure-track faculty. It is possible that the real difficulty lies not in evaluating one another per se but in competitive ranking (Smith and Walvoord, 1996). Tenure is available (at least theoretically) to whoever reaches the standard. One person's achievement of tenure does not necessarily prevent another person from achieving it. But merit pay and competitive awards give to one person at the expense of colleagues. Several departments with which we worked at the University of Cincinnati were quite willing to make tough tenure decisions, but they strongly resisted merit pay, by which a specific amount of money was supposed to be divided among department members according to their merit. The departments claimed that this merit system destroyed collegiality. They tended to even out the rewards, giving nearly the same merit pay to everyone and passing around the teaching award from year to year among a fairly large group of those deemed good teachers. The considerable autonomy that departments enjoy gives them the power to blunt the effects of reward systems that do not fit the departmental culture.

The considerable autonomy that departments enjoy gives them the power to blunt the effects of reward systems that do not fit the departmental culture.

Implications for Change

Given the characteristics of departments we have described, what are some possible avenues and strategies for change?

Change individual faculty attitudes, values, and skills

Because faculty enjoy considerable autonomy within a multiple-reward system, changes in their individual choices and values will affect departmental work. Consequently, some reform efforts focus on individual faculty (for example, provostial grants for teaching or technology or research initiatives; centrally administered teaching and learning centers; and the like).

Hold the department collectively responsible

The opposite tactic, as Wergin (1994) suggests, is to hold a department collectively responsible for its work. For example, if the department gains resources from central administration by fulfilling certain teaching goals, department members may join together to reach those goals. We saw this happen in a philosophy department that had been told by the provost that it was slated for abolishment because it was teaching so few students. Under the leadership of a strong new chair, the department worked together to get many courses approved for general education credit in an environment where there were not enough general education courses to satisfy student demand. This effort required faculty to overcome their distaste for general education courses and their impatience with the university approval procedure they had to endure to get the courses they sought.

Increase collegial interaction

Jarvis (1992) concludes, "Perhaps the single most important factor in faculty development is the concept of collegiality, what historian Page Smith calls 'the pursuit of truth in the company of friends'. . . . Development of collegiality is a central goal in all the best-known inter-institutional programs for junior faculty development, including those conducted by the Lilly Endowment, the Bush Foundation, the Central Pennsylvania Consortium, and the Great Lakes College Association" (p. 65; see also Walvoord, Hunt, Dowling, and McMahon, 1997). Bensimon, Ward, and Sanders (2000) include advice from Anna Neumann on research-based ways to foster collegiality for new faculty (pp. 123–125).

Establish new modes of quality control

The face-to-face interaction among equals that is part of traditional collegiality is difficult, given the disparity of titles and status among those who do the work in many departments, their geographical dispersion, or their different teaching schedules. So new combinations of collegial interaction with supervisory forms must be developed. An example of a change strategy that used an ingenious combination of the two forms is the method devised at the University of Cincinnati by English Department composition directors Roemer, Schultz, and Durst (1991), who set out to improve the quality of composition teaching and also to socialize adjuncts and graduate students more effectively into their teaching roles. TAs and adjuncts, who teach virtually all sections of first-year composition, are assigned to groups of three. After several meetings of all the teachers to discuss grading standards, each three-person group must meet regularly to read and evaluate each others' students' work. A portfolio of student work must receive a grade of "C" or better from two of the three readers, or the student cannot pass the course. This method encourages collegiality as the groups meet together and engage in discussions about students' work and, more broadly, about their teaching. The system also reduces the collegial group to a manageable size for people with varied schedules. At the same time, by requiring that everyone attend the meetings where grading standards are discussed and by allowing the group, rather than the individual teacher, to control whether the student passes or fails, the method provides a measure of quality control for an unstable, diverse, and largely inexperienced workforce.

Simultaneously, Roemer, Schultz, and Durst (1991) worked across a span of years, with some success, to increase the salary, benefits, and status of the adjuncts who teach composition and to provide a career path with advances in rank and pay. The two issues—quality control and justice/respect—will be crucial in the future as departments construct systems to replace the informal task delegation typical of the collegium. Routes to change include strategies that build collegiality in smaller, more specialized groups within the department combined with the supervisory tactics that allow the department to delegate work by title differentiation and to control the quality of that work.

Change hiring processes
Because the hiring process so strongly reinforces the disparity of tasks and status and because it appears to

have such long-range implications for faculty self-confidence, self-efficacy, and community, it is an obvious point of change for those who want to reform a department's work. Can disciplinary coverage be replaced or augmented by other categories for defining new positions? Can new types of specialization be an avenue for changing the department's work? The proliferation of non-tenure-track positions brings many problems, as we have noted, but it also offers the potential that slots can be created for new kinds of work. Further, large departments, in our observation, often have semiautonomous subunits that may define their work differently. An example is the extension arm of an agricultural department or the composition program in an English department. Can new quasi-independent subunits within departments take on some of the department's new work?

Build opportunities for various roles and for career-long flexibility

Fairweather's study of faculty excellence (1999), based on data from nearly 30,000 faculty at 962 institutions, suggests that only 10% of faculty are outstanding both in publishing (defined by article output) and in "instructional productivity" (defined by a combination of student credit hours generated, percentage of time spent on teaching, and use of collaborative and active learning strategies that, research suggests, will lead to more effective student learning than lectures). A route to change is to allow greater specialization so faculty can concentrate where they are most interested, talented, and/or productive. Layzell (1999) suggests two options: first, that research institutions might establish alternate routes to tenure—one focused on teaching and one on research; and second, that institutions might develop longer-term renewable contracts for faculty. The first alternative allows choice of focus at the beginning of one's career; the second offers the opportunity to change focus as one moves to a new contract.

Work with the disciplinary associations to redefine faculty work

Diamond and Adam (1995, 1998) report a series of projects at the University of Syracuse that helped disciplinary organizations construct broad definitions of scholarly work. Their efforts build upon the concepts of Boyer (1990) and Rice (1996), who proposed that "scholarship" has been defined too narrowly among faculty and must be expanded to include not only the "scholarship of discovery" in the field but also the "scholarship of teaching," of "application," and of "integration." The Carnegie project for the scholarship of teaching and learning is pushing this agenda both with disciplinary associations and with campuses (www.carnegiefoundation.org and http://aahe.ital.utexas.edu).

Change the reward system

Reviewing the literature on motivators of faculty behavior, Fairweather (1999) concludes that despite some theories that emphasize the faculty member's own psychological makeup and early socialization, the empirical evidence points to rewards as powerful determiners of faculty behavior (p. 58). One type of reward is promotion and tenure. Because they are such powerful points of attention and effort for tenure-track faculty, altering the criteria that govern promotion and tenure may be an effective strategy for change, as Diamond (2000) suggests.

One route that is being tried in a number of institutions—and is sometimes mandated by legislatures and boards—is posttenure review (Licata, 2000). Its proponents suggest using it as a focus point for chair leadership and departmental support, trying to encourage faculty members to set goals, plan strategies for their own growth, and reinvest in departmental colleagueship. Boice (1992, 1993) documented positive results when chairs and disillusioned faculty made contracts that included structured plans for coteaching with a colleague and for maintaining a catalogue of current activities and future plans for collegiality, teaching, and scholarship. Such activities fall short of adding a rung to the career ladder, but they accomplish some of the same ends—giving faculty goals to aim toward and a sense that someone encourages and appreciates their efforts.

If competitive awards seem contrary to departmental culture in ways we have suggested, change agents might consider standards-based awards, where everyone who meets a certain standard for teaching excellence would get the award (Smith and Walvoord, 1993, 1996).

Create a learning department

Given the autonomy that individual faculty enjoy in relation to the department and their tendency to define their work as individual rather than departmental, an important goal of change is to create a department in which both individual and common goals are supported—a point emphasized by the "learning organization" literature discussed in the first section. Within such a learning department, people would work together to address the key issues discussed in this section: defining the department's most appropriate work and changing that work as needed, allocating tasks appropriately among faculty and other collaborators, enhancing productivity, controlling the quality of the department's work, hiring and socializing new faculty, supporting faculty in career-long development, constructing effective reward systems, and helping people take minimally defensive stances, articulate their underlying values or theories-in-use, and learn from their own experiences.

A Case Study

Our theme in this volume has been that departments are not fossils but living entities struggling with complex problems. This section has emphasized that, given the influx of faculty who are not on a tenure track and who are increasingly dispersed geographically and chronologically, the potential of new technologies, the changing patterns of students' expectations, competition from alternative providers, and unbundling of faculty tasks, departments face difficult challenges indeed.

Lucas (2000a, pp. 34–42) presents a case study to illustrate the steps to departmental change she is recommending, but the case also nicely illustrates how a department managed change in defining its work, allocation of tasks, productivity, quality control, hiring, socialization, development, and rewards. In the Management and Marketing Department at Fairleigh Dickinson University, a small group of six faculty (out of 32 members) who viewed the department as stagnant proposed a new center that would involve partnering with industry to offer a new curriculum to students, as well as opportunities for research and consulting for faculty. They had successfully read their department's culture and potential so that they were able to generate enthusiasm for the new center. That proposal became the lever for new tasks, personnel, faculty development, and rewards. A new type of noncredit course for a new clientele of students generated revenue for the department. Committees were formed that included faculty and industry representatives, thus creating a new form of collegiality among disparate stakeholders. The members of the committees developed a new cutting-edge curriculum as well as opportunities for research and consulting that benefited both individuals and the department. Industry members were used as guest lecturers and adjuncts, thus changing the mix of faculty and introducing new values. Standards for faculty work rose. In that context during a 10-year period, a significant portion of the department retired or left, and eight new faculty were added as well as a full-time executive-in-residence funded by industry. Faculty met often to share research and for ongoing faculty development, thus helping to socialize new faculty, enhance the vitality of all faculty, and enrich collegiality.

Dynamics of change will be very different for other kinds of departments—small departments or departments in the humanities, for example. Practitioners must read their own cultures, using our observations and questions as a heuristic. But nationally, we believe that changes in departmental work, roles, and rewards present perhaps the most difficult challenge for the future and that the answer lies in finding new ways to enrich collegiality while developing new modes of task allocation, productivity, quality control, hiring, socialization, faculty development, and rewards.

Changes in departmental work, roles, and rewards present perhaps the most difficult challenge for the future, and the answer lies in finding new ways to enrich collegiality while developing new modes of task allocation, productivity, quality control, hiring, socialization, faculty development, and rewards.

Questions for Practitioners

- How does this department define its work, and who influences that definition? Could any of the defining forces exert pressure for change?
- How is the department moving in terms of its work? What was it like 10 years ago? Five years ago? What is it like now? What will be its work in the future?
- How does the department allocate tasks? Who decides which faculty will do what tasks? How might these task allocations change?
- How does the department enhance its productivity? What do members believe productivity is? What values guide the determination of productivity? Can faculty who have increased productivity be exemplars for others?

- How does the department know how well it is doing its work? Would different kinds of information help it to recognize the need for change? How can the department encourage high-quality work from members who are geographically dispersed or who work at different times of the day?
- What are the processes and criteria for new hires? Could a change in these elements bring about change in the department?
- What is the experience of a new faculty member? Could more effective socialization help the department change?
- What do faculty think they have to do to be well rewarded in this department? How do they get those messages? What are the rewards and who gives them? Could changes in the rewards or the reward processes bring about needed change in the department's work?

CONCLUSIONS: DEPARTMENTAL CHANGE

This volume has been based on our conclusion that, in the rapidly changing environment of the future, departments must change, both in what they do and in what they become, and that the key to reform is to build upon the department's own characteristics. We have analyzed those characteristics as they appear in the literature and in our own observations, and we have suggested avenues for change (see the appendix). We have emphasized several themes: Departments at their best are the flexible belt, not the fixed cog, that translates intellectual energy into multiple kinds of services to multiple constituencies. Departments are deeply influenced by their disciplines and are guided by powerful traditional values, including collegiality and autonomy. Some evidence suggests that collegial models are the most successful; however, current demands from stakeholders ask departments to change in just those ways that traditional collegiality is perhaps least able to address. Further, traditional collegial forms are stretched to the breaking point by such pressures as the increase in numbers of non-tenure-track faculty, the challenge of new technologies that enable communication across boundaries of time and space, new expectations from students and society, the rise of competitors, and the un-bundling of traditionally linked aspects of faculty work. We view departments not as fossils but as living organisms struggling to construct new forms in the face of these challenges to be more outwardly oriented, more innovative, and more entrepreneurial, to emphasize results, to collaborate more closely with a wide variety of disciplines and external agencies, and to reward effectively all types of faculty for their achievements. This analysis then leads to three agendas: local, research, and national.

A Local Agenda

The local agenda is that of the department chair, member, dean, provost, or other stakeholder who wants a particular department or set of departments to change in some way: for example, to pay more attention to undergraduate students, to raise reputation in research, or to do more work with less money. Departments differ widely. Thus, we suggest using this volume as a heuristic. Our observations will not necessarily describe the reader's own department, but will summarize some national characteristics that appear in the literature and will suggest ways of assessing one's own department. The volume supports a four-step process:

1. Decide how the department needs to change by assessing its environment and its current achievements (see "Assessing the Pressures for Departmental Change").
2. Then read the remaining sections in turn, asking what your department's characteristics suggest as change strategies. They may be the same or different from those we describe. The appendix may serve as a summary heuristic. Consider all of the six types of change strategies we summarize in the first section: change the environment, change the people, change the values, change the structure and organization, change the decision-making process, or create new structures to assume some of the department's functions.
3. Select and combine strategies in ways that fit your local situation.
4. Pay special attention to what your department needs to *be*.

The most important issue is number 4: What should the department *be?* Not all departments need to be the same, but nationally there is a visionary literature, which we summarized in the first section. It emphasizes that departments must combine new forms of collegiality with aspects of what are variously called "adhocracy" and "collegial entrepreneurialism," "quality principles," or "teamwork."

The new collegiality will have to link faculty who are increasingly diverse in background and increasingly dispersed geographically and in terms of the times of day they work. It will have to develop modes of speeding up the traditional decision-making processes in cases where swift action is needed. It will have to understand its own culture, values, and assumptions as well as the wider systems in which it operates. It will have to practice open and productive interaction that manages conflict but does not bury it. It will have to support leaders who are collaborative but who also take a forceful role in guiding change. It will have to construct effective systems of quality control, productivity, and rewards for faculty. It must develop new forms of collaboration that also nurture individual autonomy. It will have to learn from its own experience.

In addition to these new modes of collegiality, departments must be more "adhocratic" and "entrepreneurial"—that is, they need greater outward orientation, attention to demonstrable results, and flexibility in forming alliances with varied other disciplines and agencies. Gilliland (1997) observes, "Organizations that succeed in an environment of change and unpredictability promote flexibility, information access and dialogue, and risk-taking"(p. 33).

How can a department make progress toward what it needs to be? The visionary literature is heavy on describing all the wonderful qualities that departments should have but a bit thin on how a real department actually might get there. We have pointed to Angelo's steps (2000) toward a learning department. These steps are aimed at chairs, and they indicate what a department can do, operating on its own. We have suggested that new forms of university organization may be needed. What is also needed, we believe, is a research agenda and a national program of support for departments.

A Research Agenda

It is important to discover what creative and successful departments are actually doing to construct new modes of collegiality, enhance their outward orientation, attend to results, collaborate with other disciplines and agencies, or in other ways meet the challenges of their rapidly changing world. Dill (1992) calls for studies of collegiality (p. 59), and Cannon and Lonsdale (1987) urge basing theory on observation of what organizations actually do. We believe such studies are sorely needed.

Such studies may be qualitative and quantitative. Higher education needs broad-based studies on departments such as those that Smart and St. John (1996) and Smart, Kuh, and Tierney (1997) have been conducting on institutions, indicating which governance models seem linked with attributes of departmental success. Case studies and literature describing best practices are extremely thin. They most frequently appear as self-reports by department heads or change leaders. Practitioners need case studies that are well theorized and backed with evidence. Some models are found in work by V. Smith and others (1992), which, though self-reported, is shaped by theoretical framing; Tobias (1992), who studied departments that seemed especially effective in preparing undergraduate science students; Finnegan and Gamson (1996), who studied how several departments changed from an emphasis on teaching to an emphasis on research; Lucas (2000a), who presents precise information about outcomes; and Parelius and Berlin (1984), who show how two history departments addressed declining student enrollments in different ways. This research needs to be part of a national agenda and to be disseminated through a national agenda.

A State and National Agenda

At the state, system, and national levels, the overarching goal should be not merely to achieve whatever change agendas are currently most prominent, but rather to help create departments that know how to change effectively. If departments know how to change effectively, then they can change continually to meet new needs and new environments. Many state, national, and system efforts for reform currently aim at manipulating the environment outside the department, because that is where externally driven efforts can most easily operate. So programs have arisen to change the disciplinary societies or the departmental budgetary allocations, to initiate undergraduate learning communities or formal faculty development programs, to institute posttenure review of faculty or external review of departments, and to require assessment of student learning, mission-driven goals, or increased faculty teaching. All these efforts have merit. But the lesson from the University of Cincinnati is that such external mandates can simply create overload, which departments understandably resist.

We propose therefore a national initiative—a center that would:

1. Conduct research on departments and serve as a clearinghouse to disseminate information on exemplars and best practice in areas such as developing new forms of collegiality, integrating faculty peer evaluation as part of collegial systems, or dealing with increasing numbers of non-tenure-track faculty.
2. Engage and train a corps of regional, system-based, and campus-based consultants who would be available to help individual departments or colleges and universities on an ongoing basis to address their own peculiar problems and to develop more effective modes of

The over-arching goal should be not merely to achieve whatever change agendas are currently most prominent, but rather to help create departments that know how to change effectively.

governance, interaction, rewards, socialization, and the like, building on the suggestions of Bare (1980), Bolton and Boyer (1973), Crockett (1973), Hewton (1982), Kressel, Bailey, and Forman (1999), Schein (1992), and Smith, Scholten, Russell, and McCormack (1997).

3. Offer workshops and seminars, together with effective follow-up, for departmental and central administrative teams to help them understand departments, build change plans, and implement those changes.

4. Create a "safe place" for central administrators and department members to discuss and learn (Alpert, 1986).

5. Help participants learn how to study their own cultures, using some of the methods outlined by Argyris and Schön (1978), Austin (1996), Heller (1982), Senge (1990a, 1990b), and Senge, Roberts, and Ross (1994).

A state system might launch such a project for its own institutions and perhaps become a model for other states or for a national system.

If higher education hopes for broad, long-lasting change, then as individual department members, chairs, central administrators, board members, legislators, students, employers, a nation, and a higher education enterprise, we must understand departments and help them to understand their world and themselves, learn from their own actions, develop rich new forms of collegiality, be more oriented toward outside influences and outside partners, focus on results, and develop appropriate modes of hiring, socialization, faculty development, quality control, productivity, and reward for their faculty. Departments are not just resisters of change, not just silos or fortresses; they are living organizations, trying to solve the problems they perceive. It is unclear whether they can change fast enough or completely enough to remain as the dominant type of subunit in higher education or whether, in the future, they will be joined by increasing numbers of other types of subunits that take over some of the department's traditional roles. But even if that happens, departments will still need to change. The best thing that change agents can do is to respect departmental structures and cultures, and use those structures to build for change.

APPENDIX: SUMMARY OF DEPARTMENTAL CHARACTERISTICS AND AVENUES FOR CHANGE

	If Your Department Has These Characteristics:	Chairs, Members, Administrators, and Other Stakeholders Might Bring About Change Through These Strategies:
Values	Driven by five core academic values—collegiality, autonomy, academic freedom, specialization, and reason—which are powerful but may conflict with one another, are always under challenge, and may be espoused but only imperfectly realized.	• Examine the department's own values. • Look for common values among subcultures. • Analyze how values will affect desired change. • Build on the values. • Try to change the values (but remember that values change only slowly and indirectly). • Redefine the values. • Strengthen subcultures that have the desired values.
Disciplinarity	Department gains autonomy and power through its disciplinary base. Interdisciplinary collaboration is difficult. Departments differ significantly by discipline. Disciplines exercise considerable control over departmental values, norms, hiring and socialization,	• Work with disciplinary differences among departments. • Work through the disciplinary society. • Change criteria for disciplinary ranking and departmental review.

	If Your Department Has These Characteristics:	Chairs, Members, Administrators, and Other Stakeholders Might Bring About Change Through These Strategies:
	gatekeeping, and accountability in ways that rival the influence of the institution and of other external constituencies. Departments are thus multiply accountable and multiply rewarded.	• Strengthen institutional influence vis-à-vis disciplinary influence. • Change the disciplinary base of department hires. • Encourage interdisciplinary collaboration. • Create alternatives to discipline-based associations such as teaching associations. • Create a "learning department" that can reexamine its relationship to the discipline.
Relationship to Central Administration	Highly autonomous within the institution yet also subject to institutional influence through central administration's signals about mission and goals, control of information, fiscal power, influence on leaders, and ability to establish institutional structures within which departments must work.	• Build on departmental autonomy, supporting departmental change initiatives. • Establish trust, collaboration, clear signals, and shared mission. • Help the department gather and interpret information. • Use fiscal incentives tied to goals for change.

		Recommendations
		• Manage crises and deadlines. • Select and work with departmental leaders. • Create alternative structures to take over some departmental tasks. • Construct forms and processes for university governance.
Organization, Decision Making, and Interaction	Collegial modes focus on consensual decision making among peers, but departments also show aspects of oligarchic, feudal, and caste-based systems. Some evidence suggests collegial forms are best, but today's environment exerts pressure at points where collegial forms may be weakest.	• Work within collegial frames. • Address limitations of collegial systems. • Explore new models.
Leadership	Leadership is highly contextual. Department is led by untrained peer chairs with multiple allegiances and tasks, wielding ambiguous power. Leadership functions dispersed among department members.	• Chairs should analyze the culture. • Make time for strategic planning by chairs. • Change the chair's power.

	If Your Department Has These Characteristics:	**Chairs, Members, Administrators, and Other Stakeholders Might Bring About Change Through These Strategies:**
Faculty Work, Roles, and Rewards	Departmental work is defined by multiple influences and by the considerably autonomy of faculty. Departments are experimenting with new forms in the face of multiple pressures that stretch traditional modes of collegiality (see Table 1).	• Chairs should combine "consideration" with "structure-initiation." • Develop the chair's skills or leadership style. • Change individual faculty attitudes, values, and skills. • Hold the department collectively responsible. • Increase collegial interaction. • Establish new modes of quality control. • Change the hiring process. • Build opportunities for new roles and for career-long flexibility. • Work with disciplinary associations to redefine faculty work. • Change the reward system. • Help the "learning" department integrate individual and group goals.

A Vision of the Ideal Department

The ultimate goal of change: the "learning" or "collaborative" department, the "team," or the "authentically collegial" department that is enhanced by "quality" principles and that can understand its own and others' cultures and assumptions, view its environment systemically, gather and use good information, act with minimum defensiveness, allow individual freedom yet foster commitment to the well-being of the group, learn from its own experiences, and support good leaders who act consultatively yet exercise visionary leadership.

- "Build shared trust: Begin by lowering social and interpersonal barriers to change. . . .
- "Build shared motivation: Collectively determine goals worth working toward and problems worth solving—and consider the likely costs and benefits. . . .
- "Build a shared language: Develop a collective understanding of new concepts (mental models) needed for transformation. . . .
- "Design backward and work forward: Work backward from the shared vision and long-term goals to determine outcomes, strategies, and activities. . . .
- "Think and act systematically: Understand the advantages and limitations of the larger systems within which you operate and seek connections and applications to those larger worlds. . . .
- "Practice what you preach: Use what you have learned about individual and organizational learning to inform and explain your efforts and strategies. . . .
- "Do not assume, ask: Make the implicit explicit. Use assessment to focus on what matters most" (Angelo, 2000, pp. 80–86).

REFERENCES

Adams, E. M. (1997, September/October). Rationality in the academy: Why responsibility center budgeting is a wrong step down the wrong road. *Change, 29*(5), 58–61.

Alpert, D. (1986). Performance and paralysis: The organizational context of the American research university. *Journal of Higher Education, 56*(3), 76–102.

American Association of University Professors. (1995). *AAUP policy documents and reports.* Washington, DC: Author.

Anderson, G. L. (1976). Organizational diversity. In J. C. Smart and J. R. Montgomery (Eds.), *Examining departmental management.* New Directions for Institutional Research, no. 10. San Francisco: Jossey-Bass.

Anderson, M. (1992). *Imposters in the temple.* New York: Simon & Schuster. (ED 350 836)

Angelo, T. A. (2000). Transforming departments into productive learning communities. In A. F. Lucas and Associates, *Leading academic change: Essential roles for department chairs* (pp. 74–89). San Francisco: Jossey-Bass.

Argyris, C. (1982a). How learning and reasoning processes affect organizational change. In P. S. Goodman and Associates (Eds.), *Change in organizations: New perspectives on theory, research, and practice* (pp. 47–86). San Francisco: Jossey-Bass.

Argyris, C. (1982b). *Reasoning, learning, and action: Individual and organizational.* San Francisco: Jossey-Bass.

Argyris, C., and Schön, D. A. (1978). *Organizational learning: A theory of action perspective.* Reading, MA: Addison-Wesley-Longman.

Armajani, B., Heydinger, R. B., and Hutchinson, P. (1994). *A model for the reinvented higher education system.* State Policy and College Learning Series. Denver: State Higher Education Executive Officers. (ED 370 492)

Armstrong, L., Jr. (2000, June 30). *The innovator's dilemma: Creating change in a dynamic marketplace.* Paper presented at the Higher Education for a New Century Conference, University of Southern California, Los Angeles, CA.

Aronowitz, S. (1997). Academic unionism and the future of higher education. In C. Nelson (Ed.), *Will teach for food: Academic labor in crisis* (pp. 181–215). Minneapolis, MN: University of Minnesota Press.

Astin, A. W. (1985). *Achieving educational excellence* (1st ed.). San Francisco: Jossey-Bass.

Astin, A. W. (1987). Assessment, value-added, and educational excellence. In D. F. Halpern (Ed.), *Student outcomes assessment:*

What institutions stand to gain (pp. 89–107). New Directions for Higher Education, no. 59. San Francisco: Jossey-Bass.

Astin, A. W. (1993, October 21). *Higher education and the concept of community*. Fifteenth David Dodds Henry Lecture, University of Illinois–Urbana. (ED 384 279)

Astin, A. W. (1998). The changing American college student: Thirty-year trends, 1966–1996. *Review of Higher Education, 21*(2), 115–135.

Austin, A. E. (1994). Understanding and assessing faculty cultures and climates. In M. K. Kinnick (Ed.), *Providing useful information for deans and department chairs* (pp. 47–63). New Directions for Institutional Research, no. 84. San Francisco: Jossey-Bass.

Austin, A. E. (1996). *Institutional and departmental cultures: The relationship between teaching and research*. New Directions for Institutional Research, no. 90. San Francisco: Jossey-Bass.

Baldridge, J. V. (1971). *Power and conflict in the university: Research in the sociology of complex organizations*. New York: John Wiley & Sons.

Baldridge, J. V., Curtis, D. V., Ecker, G. P., and Riley, G. L. (1991). Alternative models of governance in higher education. In M. W. Peterson (Ed.), *Organization and governance in higher education* (4th ed., pp. 30–45). ASHE Reader Series. Needham Heights, MA: Ginn. (ED 109 937)

Banta, T. W. (1996). Has assessment made a difference? In T. W. Banta, J. P. Lund, K. E. Black, and F. W. Oblander (Eds.), *Assessment in practice: Putting principles to work on college campuses* (pp. 342–349). San Francisco: Jossey-Bass.

Banta, T. W., Lund, J. P., Black, K. E., and Oblander, F. W. (Eds.). (1996). *Assessment in practice: Putting principles to work on college campuses*. San Francisco: Jossey-Bass. (ED 388 163)

Bare, A. C. (1980). The study of academic department performance. *Research in Higher Education, 12*(1), 1–22.

Bare, A. C. (1986). Managerial behaviors of college chairpersons and administrators. *Research in Higher Education, 24*(2), 128–138.

Barr, R. B., and Tagg, J. (1995, November/December). From teaching to learning: A new paradigm for undergraduate education. *Change, 27*(6), 12–25.

Bates, A. W. (2000). Giving faculty ownership of technological change in the department. In A. F. Lucas and Associates, *Leading academic change: Essential roles for department chairs* (pp. 215–245). San Francisco: Jossey-Bass.

Becher, T., and Kogan, M. (1992). *Process and structure in higher education* (2nd ed.). London and New York: Routledge.

Benjamin, R., and Carroll, S. (1998). The implications of the changed environment for governance in higher education. In W. G. Tierney (Ed.), *The responsive university: Restructuring for high performance* (pp. 92–119). Baltimore: Johns Hopkins University Press. (ED 416 760)

Bennett, J. B. (1982). Ambiguity and abrupt transitions in the department chairperson's role. *Educational Record, 63*(4), 53–56.

Bensimon, E. M., and Neumann, A. (1993). *Redesigning collegiate leadership: Teams and teamwork in higher education.* Baltimore: Johns Hopkins University Press.

Bensimon, E. M., Neumann, A., and Birnbaum, R. (1989). *Making sense of administrative leadership: The "L" word in higher education.* ASHE-ERIC Higher Education Report, no. 1. Washington, DC: George Washington University, Graduate School of Education and Human Development. (ED 317 099)

Bensimon, E. M., Ward, K., and Sanders, K. (2000). *The department chair's role in developing new faculty into teachers and scholars.* Bolton, MA: Anker Press.

Bergquist, W. H. (1992). *The four cultures of the academy.* San Francisco: Jossey-Bass. (ED 343 539)

Bess, J. L. (1990, May/June). College teachers: Miscast professionals. *Change, 22*(3), 18–22.

Biglan, A. (1973a). The characteristics of subject matter in different academic areas. *Journal of Applied Psychology, 57*(3), 195–203.

Biglan, A. (1973b). Relationships between subject matter characteristics and the structure and output of university departments. *Journal of Applied Psychology, 57*(3), 204–213.

Birnbaum, R. (1988). *How colleges work: The cybernetics of academic organization and leadership.* San Francisco: Jossey-Bass. (ED 301 114)

Blackburn, R. T., Horowitz, S. M., Edington, D. W., and Klos, D. (1986). University faculty and administrator response to job strains. *Research in Higher Education, 25*(1), 31–41.

Blandy, R., Dawkins, P., Gannicott, K., Kain, P., Kasper, W., and Kriegler, R. (1985). *Structural chaos: The process of productivity advance.* New York: Oxford University Press.

Boice, R. (1991). New faculty as teachers. *Journal of Higher Education, 62,* 150–173.

Boice, R. (1992). *The new faculty member: Supporting and fostering professional development.* San Francisco: Jossey-Bass. (ED 343 537)

Boice, R. (1993). Primal origins and later correctives for midcareer disillusionment. In M. J. Finkelstein and M. W. LaCelle-Peterson (Eds.), *Developing senior faculty as teachers*. New Directions for Teaching and Learning, no. 55. San Francisco: Jossey-Bass.

Bolman, L. G., and Deal, T. E. (1991). *Reframing organizations: Artistry, choice, and leadership*. San Francisco: Jossey-Bass. (ED 332 345)

Bolton, C. K., and Boyer, R. K. (1973). Organizational development for academic departments. *Journal of Higher Education, 44*(5), 352–369.

Bowen, H., and Schuster, J. H. (1986). *American professors: A national resource imperiled*. New York: Oxford University Press. (ED 272 086)

Boyer, E. L. (1990). *Scholarship reconsidered: Priorities of the professoriate*. Princeton, NJ: Carnegie Foundation for the Advancement of Teaching. (ED 326 149)

Braxton, J. M., and Hargens, L. L. (1996). Variation among academic disciplines: Analytical frameworks. In J. C. Smart (Ed.), *Higher education: Handbook of theory and research* (*Vol. 11,* pp. 1–46). New York: Agathon Press. (ED 393 365)

Bresser, R. K. (1984). The context of university departments: Differences between fields of higher and lower levels of paradigm development. *Research in Higher Education, 20*(1), 3–15.

Brown, J. S. (1997, January/February). On becoming a learning organization. *About Campus, 1*(6), 5–10.

Brown, W. R. (1982). *Academic politics*. University, AL: University of Alabama Press. (ED 229 677)

Burke, D. L. (1995, January/February). *Plus ça change:* An academic workforce in transition. *Academe, 81*(1), 7–11.

Cameron, K. S., and Ettington, D. R. (1988). The conceptual foundations of organizational culture. In J. C. Smart (Ed.), *Higher education: Handbook of theory and research* (*Vol. 4,* pp. 356–396). New York: Agathon Press.

Cannon, R. A., and Lonsdale, A. J. (1987). A "muddled array of models": Theoretical and organisational perspectives on change and development in higher education. *Higher Education, 16*(1), 21–32.

Carey, A. K., Soled, S., and Walvoord, B. E. (1998, January 30). *Collegiality and community: Developing a collaborative and productive department culture*. Presentation at the 6th American Association for Higher Education Forum on Faculty Roles and Rewards, Orlando, FL. (Audiotape Recording No. 805–295–0504m, Mobiltape Company, 24730 Avenue Tibbitts, Suite 170, Valencia, CA 91355)

Carroll, J. B. (1991). Career paths of department chairs: A national perspective. *Research in Higher Education, 32*(6), 669–688.

Carroll, J. B., and Gmelch, W. H. (1992). *A factor-analytic investigation of role types and profiles of higher education department chairs.* Presentation at the Annual Meeting of the American Educational Research Association, April 20–24, Washington, DC. (ED 345 629)

Chaffee, E. E., and Sherr, L. A. (1992). *Quality: Transforming postsecondary education.* ASHE-ERIC Higher Education Report, no. 3. Washington, DC: George Washington University, Graduate School of Education and Human Development. (ED 351 922)

Clark, B. R. (1970). *The distinctive college: Antioch, Reed, and Swarthmore.* Chicago: Aldine.

Clark, B. R. (1987). *The academic life: Small worlds, different worlds.* Princeton, NJ: Carnegie Foundation for the Advancement of Teaching. (ED 299 902)

Clark, B. R. (2000, January/February). Collegial entrepreneurialism in proactive universities: Lessons from Europe. *Change, 32*(1), 10–19.

Clark, M. E., and Wawrytko, S. A. (Eds.). (1990). *Rethinking the curriculum: Toward an integrated, interdisciplinary college education.* New York: Greenwood Press.

Colton, J. (1995). The role of the department in the groves of academe. In A. L. De Neef and C. D. Goodwin (Eds.), *The academic's handbook* (2nd ed., pp. 315–333). Durham, NC: Duke University Press.

Conrad, C. F. (1978). A grounded theory of academic change. *Sociology of Education, 51*(2), 101–102.

Conrad, C. F., and Haworth, J. G. (1992–93). Master's programs and contextual planning. *Planning for Higher Education, 21*(2): 12–18.

Costanza, R. (1990). Escaping the overspecialization trap: Creating incentives for a transdisciplinary synthesis. In M. E. Clark and S. A. Wawrytko (Eds.) *Rethinking the curriculum: Toward an integrated, interdisciplinary college education* (pp. 95–106). New York: Greenwood Press.

Crockett, C. (1973). The higher education institute: A vehicle for change. *Journal of Higher Education, 44*(5), 414–425.

Crothers, C. (1991). The internal structure of sociology departments: The role of graduate students and other groups. *Teaching Sociology, 19*(3), 333–343.

Dahlgren, L. O., and Pramling, I. (1985). Conceptions of knowledge, professionalism and contemporary problems in some professional academic subcultures. *Studies in Higher Education, 10*(2), 163–173.

David, P. (1997, October 4). Universities: Inside the knowledge factory. *The Economist.* (Reprints available from The Economist Newspaper Group, Reprints Dept., 111 W. 57th Street, New York, NY 10019, 212–541–5730)

Davis, R. H., Strand, R., Alexander, L. T., and Hussain, M. N. (1982). The impact of organizational and innovator variables on instructional innovation in higher education. *Journal of Higher Education, 53*(5), 568–586.

Deetz, S. A. (1992). Departmental leadership and departmental culture. In M. Hickson III and D. W. Stacks (Eds.), *Effective communication for academic chairs* (pp. 1–22). SUNY Series in Speech Communication. Albany, NY: State University of New York Press. (ED 351 989)

Diamond, R. M. (1993). Changing priorities and the faculty reward system. In R. M. Diamond and B. E. Adam (Eds.), *Recognizing faculty work: reward systems for the year 2000* (pp. 5–12). New Directions for Higher Education, no. 81. San Francisco: Jossey-Bass.

Diamond, R. M. (1999). *Aligning faculty rewards with institutional mission: Statements, policies, and guidelines.* Bolton, MA: Anker Press. (ED 432 178)

Diamond, R. M. (2000). The departmental statement on promotion and tenure: A key to successful leadership. In A. F. Lucas and Associates, *Leading academic change: Essential roles for department chairs* (pp. 95–106). San Francisco: Jossey-Bass.

Diamond, R. M., and Adam, B. E. (1995). *The disciplines speak: Rewarding the scholarly, professional, and creative work of faculty.* Washington, DC: American Association for Higher Education. (ED 406 957)

Diamond, R. M., and Adam, B. E. (1998). *Changing priorities at research universities: 1991–1996.* Syracuse, NY: Syracuse University, Center for Institutional Development.

Diamond, R. M., and Adam, B. E. (2000). *The disciplines speak II: More statements on rewarding the scholarly, professional, and creative work of faculty.* Washington, DC: American Association for Higher Education.

Dill, D. D. (1984). The nature of administrative behavior in higher education. *Educational Administration Quarterly, 20*(3), 69–99.

Dill, D. D. (1992). Quality by design: Toward a framework for academic quality management. In J. C. Smart (Ed.), *Higher education: Handbook of theory and research* (*Vol. 8,* pp. 37–83). New York: Agathon Press. (ED 369 341)

Dill, W. R. (1998, July/August). Specialized accreditation: An idea whose time has come? Or gone? *Change, 30*(4), 18–25.

Easterby-Smith, M. (1987). Change and innovation in higher education: A role for corporate strategy? *Higher Education, 16*(1), 37–52.

Edwards, R. (1993, December). Bringing the "team approach" to general studies. *AAHE Bulletin, 46*(4), 12–16.

Edwards, R. (1999, September/October). How does it fit into the university reform agenda? *Change, 31*(5), 16–27.

Epstein, L. D. (1974). *Governing the university: The campus and public interest.* San Francisco: Jossey-Bass.

Ewell, P. T. (1997, December). Organizing for learning: A new imperative. *AAHE Bulletin, 50*(4), 3–6.

Ewell, P. T. (1998). Achieving high performance: The policy dimension. In W. G. Tierney (Ed.), *The responsive university: Restructuring for high performance* (pp. 120–161). Baltimore: Johns Hopkins University Press. (ED 416 760)

Ewell, P. T. (1999, January/February). From the states: National survey of good practices. *Assessment Update, 11*(1), 14–15.

Fairweather, J. (1999). The highly productive faculty member. In W. G. Tierney (Ed.), *Faculty productivity: Facts, fictions, and issues* (pp. 55–98). New York and London: Garland Press.

Falk, G. (1979). The academic department chairmanship and role conflict. *Improving College and University Teaching, 27*(2), 79–86.

Filan, G. L. (1999). The need for leadership training: The evolution of the chair academy. In R. Gillett-Karam (Ed.), *Preparing department chairs for their leadership roles* (pp. 47–55). New Directions for Community Colleges, no. 105. San Francisco: Jossey-Bass.

Fink, L. D. (1992). Orientation programs for new faculty. In M. D. Sorcinelli and A. E. Austin (Eds.), *Developing new and junior faculty* (pp. 39–49). New Directions for Teaching and Learning, no. 50. San Francisco: Jossey-Bass.

Finnegan, D. E., and Gamson, Z. F. (1996). Disciplinary adaptations to research culture in comprehensive institutions. *Review of Higher Education, 19*(2), 141–177.

Foote, E. (1999). Sources and information on midlevel managers in the community college. In R. Gillett-Karam (Ed.), *Preparing department chairs for their leadership roles* (pp. 75–82). New Directions for Community Colleges, no. 105. San Francisco: Jossey-Bass.

Francis, J. G., and Hampton, M. C. (1999). Resourceful responses: The adaptive research university and the drive to market. *Journal of Higher Education, 70*(6), 625–641.

Froh, R. C., Menges, R. J., and Walker, C. J. (1993). Revitalizing faculty work through intrinsic rewards. In R. M. Diamond and B. E. Adam (Eds.), *Recognizing faculty work: Reward systems for the year 2000* (pp. 87–95). New Directions for Higher Education, no. 81. San Francisco: Jossey-Bass.

Fulton, R. D. (2000, May/June). The plight of part-timers in higher education: Some ruminations and suggestions. *Change, 32*(3), 38–43.

Gappa, J. M. (1997). Two faculties or one? The conundrum of part-timers in a bifurcated workforce. *AAHE New Pathways.* Working Paper, no. 6. Washington, DC: American Association for Higher Education. (ED 424 817)

Gappa, J. M., and Leslie, D. W. (1993). *The invisible faculty: Improving the status of part-timers in higher education.* San Francisco: Jossey-Bass. (ED 358 756)

Gardiner, L. F. (2000). Monitoring and improving educational quality in the academic department. In A. F. Lucas and Associates, *Leading academic change: Essential roles for department chairs* (pp. 165–194). San Francisco: Jossey-Bass. (ED 424 817)

Gardiner, L. F., Anderson, C., and Cambridge, B. L. (Eds.). (1997). *Learning through assessment: A resource guide for higher education.* Washington, DC: American Association for Higher Education. (ED 414 814)

Gillett-Karam, R. (Ed.). (1999). *Preparing department chairs for their leadership roles.* New Directions for Community Colleges, no. 105. San Francisco: Jossey-Bass. (ED 428 812)

Gilley, J. W., Fulmer, K. A., and Reithlingshoefer, S. J. (1986). *Searching for academic excellence.* New York: American Council on Education/Macmillan.

Gilliland, M. W. (1997, May/June). Organizational change and tenure: We can learn from the corporate experience. *Change, 29*(3), 30–33.

Gmelch, W. H. (1995). Department chairs under siege: Resolving the web of conflict. In S. Holton (Ed.), *Conflict management in higher education.* New Directions for Higher Education, no. 92. San Francisco: Jossey-Bass.

Gmelch, W. H., and Miskin, V. D. (1993). *Leadership skills for department chairs.* Bolton, MA: Anker Press. (ED 363 257)

Gmelch, W. H., Wilke, P. K., and Lovrich, N. P. (1986). Dimensions of stress among university faculty: Factor-analytic results from a national study. *Research in Higher Education, 24*(3), 266–286.

Goethals, G. R., and Frantz, C. M. (1998). Thinking seriously about paying for college. *AAHE Bulletin, 51*(2), 3–7.

Green, K. C., and Gilbert, S. W. (1995). Content, communications, productivity, and the role of information technology in higher education. *Change, 27*(2), 8–18.

Green, M. F. (1997). *Transforming higher education: Views from leaders around the world.* Phoenix, AZ: American Council on Education/Oryx.

Groner, N. E. (1978). Leadership situations in academic departments: Relations among measures of situational favorableness and control. *Research in Higher Education, 8*(2), 125–143.

Guskin, A. E. (1994, September/October). Restructuring the role of faculty. *Change, 26*(5), 16–25.

Guskin, A. E., and Bassis, M. (1985). Leadership styles and institutional renewal. In R. M. Davis (Ed.), *Leadership and institutional renewal,* (pp. 13–22). New Directions for Higher Education, no. 49. San Francisco: Jossey-Bass.

Hackman, J. D. (1985). Power and centrality in the allocation of resources in colleges and universities. *Administrative Science Quarterly, 30*(1), 61–77.

Hardy, C., Langley, A., Mintzberg, H., and Rose, J. (1984). Strategy formation in the university setting. In J. L. Bess (Ed.), *College and university organization: Insights from the behavioral sciences* (pp. 169–210). New York: New York University Press.

Hayward, P. C. (1986). A discriminant analytic test of Biglan's theoretical distinction between biology and English department chairpersons. *Research in Higher Education, 25*(2), 136–146.

Hearn, J. C. (1999). Pay and performance in the university: An examination of faculty salaries. *Review of Higher Education, 22*(4), 391–410.

Hecht, I., Higgerson, M. L., Gmelch, W. H., and Tucker, A. (1999). *The department chair as academic leader.* Phoenix, AZ: Oryx. (ED 423 815)

Heller, J. F. (1982). *Increasing faculty and administrative effectiveness.* San Francisco: Jossey-Bass. (ED 217 746)

Hemphill, J. K. (1955). Leadership behavior associated with the administrative reputations of college departments. *Journal of Educational Psychology, 46*(6), 385–401.

Heterick, R. C., Jr., Mingle, J. R., and Twigg, C. A. (1997). *The public policy implications of a global learning infrastructure.* Report from a Joint NLII-SHEEO Symposium, November 13–14, Denver, CO.

Hewton, E. (1982). *Rethinking educational change: A case for diplomacy.* Guildford, Surrey, UK: Society for Research into Higher Education. (ED 217 762)

Hirst, L., and Blomquist, D. (1994). *Partnerships improve teaching and learning.* Paper presented at the 18th National Conference on Successful College Teaching, February 26–28, Orlando, FL.

Hobbs, W. C., and Anderson, G. L. (1971). The operation of academic departments. *Management Science, 18,* 134–144.

Holland, J. L. (1973). *Making vocational choices: A theory of careers.* Englewood Cliffs, NJ: Prentice Hall.

Huber, B. J. (1994). The responsibilities of and compensations for being a department chair: Findings from the MLA's 1989–90 survey of foreign language programs. *ADFL Bulletin, 25*(3), 107–118.

Inayatullah, S., and Gidley, J. (2000, March/April). Trends transforming the universities of this century: Virtualize, disappear, or transform. *On the Horizon, 8*(2), 1–6.

Institute for Research in Higher Education (1997, May/June). Adding it up: The price-income squeeze in higher education. *Change, 29*(3), 45–48.

Janzow, F. T., Hinni, J. B., and Johnson, J. R. (1996). Administering the curriculum. In J. G. Gaff, J. L. Ratcliff, and Associates (Eds.), *Handbook of the undergraduate curriculum: A comprehensive guide to purposes, structures, practices, and change* (pp. 497–512). San Francisco: Jossey-Bass. (ED 118 744)

Jarvis, D. K. (1992). *Junior faculty development: A handbook.* New York: Modern Language Association of America.

Jordan, J. M., Meador, M., and Walters, S.J.K. (1989). Academic research productivity, department size and organization: Further results. *Economics of Education Review, 8*(4), 345–352.

Kahn, S. (1996). Awards to groups: The University of Wisconsin System's departmental teaching award. In M. Svinicki and R. J. Menges (Eds.), *Honoring exemplary teaching* (pp. 11–16). New Directions for Teaching and Learning, no. 65. San Francisco: Jossey-Bass.

Karseth, B. (1995). The emergence of new educational programs in the university. *Review of Higher Education, 18*(2), 195–216.

Katz, M. B. (1987). *Reconstructing American education.* Cambridge, MA: Harvard University Press.

Keller, G. (1989). Shotgun marriage: The growing connection between academic management and faculty governance. In J. H. Schuster, L. H. Miller, and Associates (Eds.), *Governing tomorrow's campus: Perspectives and agendas* (pp. 133–140). New York: American Council on Education/Macmillan. (ED 311 819)

Kennedy, D. (1997). *Academic duty.* Cambridge, MA: Harvard University Press. (ED 413 805)

Kerr, S., and Jermier, J. M. (1978). Substitutes for leadership: Their meaning and measurement. *Organizational Behavior and Human Performance, 22,* 375–403.

Klein, T. (1985). What one academic department in a university learned from general education reform. *Liberal Education, 71*(4), 327–334.

Knight, W. H., and Holden, M. C. (1985). Leadership and the perceived effectiveness of department chairpersons. *Journal of Higher Education, 56*(6), 677–690.

Kozma, R. B. (1985). A grounded theory of instructional innovation in higher education. *Journal of Higher Education, 56*(3), 300–319.

Kressel, K., Bailey, J., and Forman, S. (1999). Psychological consultation in higher education: Lessons from a university faculty development center. *Journal of Educational and Psychological Consultation, 10*(1), 51–82.

Kuh, G. D., and Whitt, E. J. (1988). *The invisible tapestry: Culture in American colleges and universities.* ASHE-ERIC Higher Education Report, no. 1. Washington, DC: Association for the Study of Higher Education. (ED 299 934)

Lamber, J., Ardizzone, T., Dworkin, T., Guskin, S., Olsen, D., Parnell, P., and Thelen, D. (1993). A "community of scholars"? Conversations among mid-career faculty at a public research university. *To Improve the Academy 12,* 13–26.

Lane, J.-E. (1985). Academic profession in academic organization. *Higher Education, 14*(3), 241–268.

Lattuca, L. R., and Stark, J. S. (1994). Will disciplinary perspectives impede curricular reform? *Journal of Higher Education, 65*(4), 401–426.

Layzell, D. T. (1999). Linking performance to funding outcomes at the state level for public institutions of higher education: Past, present, and future. *Research in Higher Education, 40*(2), 233–246.

Lazerson, M., Wagener, U., and Shumanis, N. (2000, May/June). What makes a revolution? *Change, 32*(3): 12–19.

Leslie, D. W. (1973, December). The status of the department chairmanship in university organization. *AAUP Bulletin, 59*(4), 419–426.

Levin, H. M. (1991). Raising productivity in higher education. *Journal of Higher Education, 62*(3), 241–262.

Levine, A. (1980). *Why innovations fail.* Albany, NY: State University of New York Press.

Levine, A., and Cureton, J. S. (1998, May/June). Collegiate life: An obituary. *Change, 30*(3), 14–17+.

Licata, C. (2000). Post-tenure review. In A. F. Lucas and Associates, *Leading academic change: Essential roles for department chairs* (pp. 107–137). San Francisco: Jossey-Bass.

Lincoln, Y. S. (1986). *Indigenous efforts at individualizing program review: A case study.* Paper presented at the Annual Meeting of the Association for the Study of Higher Education, February 20–23, San Antonio, TX. (ED 268 892)

Loftis, J. E. (1995, Spring). Engineering democracy: Departmental organization. *ADE Bulletin, 110,* 20–23.

Louis, K. S., Anderson, M. S., and Rosenberg, L. (1995). Academic misconduct and values: The department's influence. *Review of Higher Education, 18*(4), 393–422.

Lucas, A. F. (1989). Motivating faculty to improve the quality of teaching. In A. F. Lucas (Ed.), *The department chairperson's role in enhancing college teaching* (pp. 5–15). New Directions for Teaching and Learning, no. 37. San Francisco: Jossey-Bass.

Lucas, A. F. (1994). *Strengthening departmental leadership: A team-building guide for chairs in colleges and universities.* San Francisco: Jossey-Bass.

Lucas, A. F. (2000a). A collaborative model for leading academic change. In A. F. Lucas and Associates, *Leading academic change: Essential roles for department chairs* (pp. 33–54). San Francisco: Jossey-Bass.

Lucas, A. F. (2000b). A teamwork approach to change in the academic department. In A. F. Lucas and Associates, *Leading academic change: Essential roles for department chairs* (pp. 7–32). San Francisco: Jossey-Bass.

Lucas, A. F. (Ed.). (1989). *The department chairperson's role in enhancing college teaching.* New Directions for Teaching and Learning, no. 37. San Francisco: Jossey-Bass.

Lucas, A. F., and Associates. (2000). *Leading academic change: Essential roles for department chairs.* San Francisco: Jossey-Bass.

Lueddeke, G. R. (1999). Toward a constructivist framework for guiding change and innovation in higher education. *Journal of Higher Education, 70*(3), 235–260.

Machung, A. (1998, July/August). Playing the rankings game. *Change, 30*(4), 12–16.

Manns, C. L., and March, J. G. (1978, December). Financial adversity, internal competition, and curriculum change in a university. *Administrative Science Quarterly, 23*(4), 541–552.

Marchese, T. (1998). Not-so-distant competitors: How new providers are remaking the postsecondary marketplace. *AAHE Bulletin, 1997–1998,* 50. (ED 425 677)

Massy, W. F. (1996, Winter). New thinking on academic restructuring. *AGB Priorities,* no. 6. Washington, DC: Association of Governing Boards.

Massy, W. F., Wilger, A. K., and Colbeck, C. (1994, July/August). Overcoming "hollowed" collegiality. *Change, 26*(4), 10–20.

Massy, W. F., and Zemsky, R. (1995). *Using information technology to enhance academic productivity.* Washington, DC: Educom.

McAdams, R. P. (1997). Revitalizing the department chair. *AAHE Bulletin, 49*(6), 10–13.

McCarthy, M. (1972). *Correlates of effectiveness among academic department heads.* Unpublished doctoral dissertation, Kansas State University.

McKeachie W. J. (1976). Reactions from a former department chairman. In J. C. Smart and J. R. Montgomery (Eds.), *Examining departmental management.* New Directions for Institutional Research, no. 10. San Francisco: Jossey-Bass.

Mets, L. A. (1995, Summer). Program review in academic departments. In R. J. Barak and L. A. Mets (Eds.), *Using Academic Review* (pp. 19–36). New Directions for Institutional Research, no. 86. San Francisco: Jossey-Bass.

Michael, S. O. (1998). Restructuring U. S. higher education: Analyzing models for academic program review and discontinuation. *Review of Higher Education, 21*(4), 377–404.

Middaugh, M. (1995–96, Winter). Closing in on faculty productivity measures. *Planning for Higher Education, 24*(2), 1–12.

Mitchell, M. B. (1987). The process of department leadership. *Review of Higher Education, 11*(2), 161–176.

Mohrman, K. (1989). Principals and agents in campus governance. In J. H. Schuster, L. H. Miller, and Associates (Eds.), *Governing tomorrow's campus: Perspectives and agendas* (pp. 59–84). New York: American Council on Education/Macmillan. (ED 311 819)

Moxley, J. M., and Olson, G. A. (1990). The English chair: Scholar or bureaucrat? *Thought & Action, 6*(1), 51–58.

National Center for Education Statistics. (1996a). *The condition of education, 1996.* Washington, DC: Government Printing Office.

National Center for Education Statistics. (1996b). *The digest of educational statistics, 1996.* Washington, DC: Government Printing Office.

National Center for Education Statistics. (1997a). *The condition of education, 1997.* Washington, DC: Government Printing Office.

National Center for Education Statistics. (1997b). *Current funds, revenues, and expenditures of institutions of higher education: Fiscal years 1987 through 1995.* Report 97–441. Washington, DC: Government Printing Office.

National Center for Education Statistics. (1997c). *Federal support for education: Fiscal years 1980 to 1997.* Report 97–383. Washington, DC: Government Printing Office.

National Center for Education Statistics. (1998). *The condition of education, 1998.* Washington, DC: Government Printing Office.

Nelson, C. (Ed.). (1997). *Will teach for food: Academic labor in crisis.* Minneapolis, MN: University of Minnesota Press.

Neumann, A., and Larson, R. S. (1997). Enhancing the leadership factor in planning. In M. W. Peterson, D. D. Dill, L. A. Mets, and Associates, *Planning and management for a changing environment* (pp. 191–203). San Francisco: Jossey-Bass.

Nichols, J. O. (1995a). *Assessment case studies: Common issues in implementation with various campus approaches to resolution.* New York: Agathon Press.

Nichols, J. O. (1995b). *The departmental guide and record book for student outcomes assessment and institutional effectiveness* (2nd ed.). New York: Agathon Press. (ED 410 796)

Nichols, J. O. (1995c). *A practitioner's handbook for institutional effectiveness and student outcomes assessment implementation* (3d ed.). New York: Agathon Press. (ED 410 798)

O'Connell, J. (1998, March-April). Harnessing the new individualism. *Workplace Visions,* 4–6.

Olsen, D. (1992). Interviews with exiting faculty: Why do they leave? *To Improve the Academy, 11,* 35–47. (ED 392 382)

Olsen, D., and Sorcinelli, M. D. (1992). The pretenure years: A longitudinal perspective. In M. D. Sorcinelli and A. E. Austin (Eds.), *Developing new and junior faculty* (pp. 15–25). New Directions for Teaching and Learning, no. 50. San Francisco: Jossey-Bass.

Parelius, R. J., and Berlin, W. (1984, July/August). Two history departments dealing with the dynamics of decline. *Change, 16*(5), 12–17.

Pascarella, E. T., and Terenzini, P. T. (1991). *How college affects students: Findings and insights from twenty years of research.* San Francisco: Jossey-Bass. (ED 330 287)

Perrow, C. (1986). *Complex organizations: A critical essay* (3rd ed.). New York: McGraw-Hill.

Peterson, M. W., and White, T. H. (1992). Faculty and administrator perceptions of their environments: Different views or different models of organization? *Research in Higher Education, 33*(2), 177–204.

Pew Higher Education Roundtable. (1996, February). Double agent. *Pew Policy Perspectives, 6*(3), 1–12. (ED 394 366)

Pike, G. R. (2000, March/April). Rethinking the role of assessment. *About Campus, 5*(1), 11–19.

Plater, W. M. (1995). Future work: Faculty time in the 21st century. *Change, 27*(3), 23–33.

Pollicino, E. (1996). *Faculty satisfaction with institutional support as a complex concept: Collegiality, workload, autonomy.* Paper presented at the Annual Meeting of the American Educational Research Association, April 8–13, New York, NY. (ED 394 428)

Privateer, P. M. (1999). Academic technology and the future of higher education: Strategic paths taken and not taken. *Journal of Higher Education, 70*(1), 60–79.

Public Agenda, the National Center for Public Policy and Higher Education, the Consortium for Policy Research in Education, and the National Center for Postsecondary Improvement. (2000). *Great expectations: How the public and parents—White, African, and Hispanic—view higher education.* www.highereducation.org and www.publicagenda.org.

Ramey, V. J., and Dodge, L. D. (1983). Some empirical issues in research on academic departments: Homogeneity, aggregation, and level of analysis. *Research in Higher Education, 18*(2), 409–419.

Ramsden, P. (1998). *Learning to lead in higher education.* New York: Routledge. (ED 423 766)

Reisberg, L. (1998, May 29). Most Americans overestimate college costs, poll shows. *Chronicle of Higher Education,* A39.

Reiser, S. J. (1995). Linking excellence in teaching to departments' budgets. *Academic Medicine, 70*(4), 272–275.

Reynolds, A. (1992). Charting the changes in junior faculty. *Journal of Higher Education, 63*(6), 637–652.

Rhoads, R. A., and Tierney, W. G. (1992). *Cultural leadership in higher education.* University Park, PA: Pennsylvania State University, National Center on Postsecondary Teaching, Learning, and Assessment. (ED 357 708)

Rice, R. E. (1996). Making a place for the new American scholar. *New pathways: Faculty career and employment for the 21st century.* Working Paper Series, Inquiry No. 1. Washington, DC: American Association for Higher Education. (ED 424 812)

Rice, R. E., and Austin, A. E. (1988, March/April). High faculty morale: What exemplary colleges do right. *Change, 20*(2), 50–58.

Robertson, D. (1993). *A dictionary of modern politics* (2nd ed.). London: Europa Publications.

Roemer, M., Schultz, L., and Durst, R. (1991). Portfolios and the process of change. *College Composition and Communication, 42*(4), 455–469. (ED 424 812)

Rosch, T. A., and Reich, J. N. (1996). The enculturation of new faculty in higher education: A comparative investigation of three academic departments. *Research in Higher Education, 37*(1), 115–131.

Ruscio, K. P. (1987a). The distinctive scholarship of the selective liberal arts college. *Journal of Higher Education, 58*(2), 205–222. (ED 352 735)

Ruscio, K. P. (1987b). Many sectors, many professions. In B. R. Clark (Ed.), *The academic profession: National disciplinary and institutional settings* (pp. 331–368). Los Angeles: University of California Press. (ED 265 796)

Rutherford, D., Fleming, W., and Mathias, H. (1985). Strategies for change in higher education: Three political models. *Higher Education, 14*(4), 433–445.

Ryan, D. W. (1972). The internal organization of academic departments. *Journal of Higher Education, 43*(6), 464–482.

Salancik, G. R., and Pfeffer, J. (1974, December). The bases and use of power in organizational decision making: The case of a university. *Administrative Science Quarterly, 19*(4), 453–473.

Schein, E. H. (1992). *Organizational culture and leadership* (2nd ed.). San Francisco: Jossey-Bass.

Schmidt, P. (1998a, June 19). Governors want fundamental changes in colleges, question place of tenure. *Chronicle of Higher Education,* A38.

Schmidt, P. (1998b, July 24). States increasingly link budgets to performance. *Chronicle of Higher Education,* A26.

Schmidt, P. (2000, June 30). States set a course for higher-education systems. *Chronicle of Higher Education,* A27.

Schoenfeld, C. (1994, Winter). Campus cultures in conflict. *CUPA Journal, 45*(4), 29–33.

Schuster, J. (2000, June 29). *Tenure reform and academic freedom: Where are we heading?* Paper presented at the Higher Education for a New Century Conference, University of Southern California, Los Angeles, CA.

Seagren, A. T., Creswell, J. W., and Wheeler, D. W. (1993). *The department chair: New roles, responsibilities, and challenges.* ASHE-ERIC Higher Education Report, no. 1. Washington, DC: George Washington University, Graduate School of Education and Human Development. (ED 363 164)

Seagren, A. T., Wheeler, D. W., Creswell, J. W., Miller, M. T., and Van Horn–Grassmeyer, K. (1994). *Academic leadership in community colleges.* Lincoln: University of Nebraska Press. (ED 373 810)

Senge, P. M. (1990a). *The fifth discipline: The art and practice of the learning organization.* New York: Doubleday Currency.

Senge, P. M. (1990b). The leader's new work: Building learning organizations. *Sloan Management Review, 32*(1), 7–23.

Senge, P. M. (1996). Rethinking leadership in the learning organization. *The Systems Thinker, 7*(1), 1–7.

Senge, P. M. (2000). The academy as learning community: Contradiction in terms or realizable future? In A. F. Lucas and Associates, *Leading academic change: Essential roles for department chairs* (pp. 275–300). San Francisco: Jossey-Bass.

Senge, P. M., Roberts, C., and Ross, R. B. (1994). *The fifth discipline fieldbook: Strategies and tools for building a learning organization.* New York: Doubleday.

Seymour, D. T. (1988). *Developing academic programs: The climate for innovation.* ASHE-ERIC Higher Education Report, no. 3. Washington, DC: Association for the Study of Higher Education. (ED 305 015)

Simpson, W. A., and Sperber, W. E. (1984). A new type of cost analysis for planners in academic departments. *Planning for Higher Education, 12*(3), 13–17.

Smart, J. C., and Elton, C. F. (1982). Validation of the Biglan model. *Research in Higher Education, 17*(3), 213–229.

Smart, J. C., Kuh, G. D., and Tierney, W. G. (1997). The role of institutional cultures and decision approaches in promoting organizational effectiveness in two-year colleges. *Journal of Higher Education, 68*(3), 256–281.

Smart, J. C., and St. John, E. P. (1996). Organizational culture and effectiveness in higher education: A test of the "culture type" and "strong culture" hypotheses. *Educational Evaluation and Policy Analysis, 18*(3), 219–241.

Smelser, N. J., and Content, R. (1980). *The changing academic market: General trends and a Berkeley case study.* Berkeley, CA: University of California Press. (ED 207 454)

Smith, B., Scholten, I., Russell, A., and McCormack, P. (1997, April). Integrating student assessment practices: The significance of collaborative partnerships for curriculum and professional development in a university department. *Higher Education Research and Development, 16*(1), 69–86.

Smith, H. L., and Walvoord, B. E. (1993). Certifying teaching excellence: An alternative paradigm to the teaching award. *AAHE Bulletin, 46*(2), 3–5+.

Smith, H. L., and Walvoord, B. E. (1996). The certification paradigm. In M. Svinicki and R. Menges (Eds.), *Honoring exemplary teaching* (pp. 17–23). New Directions for Teaching and Learning, no. 65. San Francisco: Jossey-Bass.

Smith, P. (1990). *Killing the spirit: Higher education in America.* New York: Viking Penguin.

Smith, V. R., Ahmed, E., Brunton, B., Kohen, A. I., Milliman, S., Rosser, M., and Stevens, D. (1992). Reviewing an economics curriculum in the context of university-wide reforms. *JGE: The Journal of General Education, 41,* 160–176.

Stark, J. S., and Lattuca, L. R. (1997). *Shaping the college curriculum: Academic plans in action.* Needham Heights, MA: Allyn and Bacon.

Stoecker, J. L. (1993). The Biglan classification revisited. *Research in Higher Education, 34*(4), 451–464.

Sykes, C. J. (1988). *ProfScam: Professors and the demise of higher education.* New York: St. Martin's Press.

Theus, K. T., and Billingsley, J. M. (1992). *An analysis of organizational change: A contingency model of environmental influence.* Paper presented at the Annual Meeting of the Speech Communication Association, October 29–November 1, Chicago, IL. (ED 353 625)

Thomas, C., and Simpson, D. J. (1995). Community, collegiality, and diversity: Is there a conflict of interest in the professoriate? *Journal of Negro Education, 64*(1), 1–5.

Tierney, W. G. (1997). Organizational socialization in higher education. *Journal of Higher Education, 68*(1), 1–16.

Tierney, W. G. (1999). *Building the responsive campus: Creating high performance colleges and universities.* Thousand Oaks, CA: Sage. (ED 428 620)

Tierney, W. G. (Ed.). (1999). *Faculty productivity: Facts, fictions, and issues.* New York: Garland Press. (ED 428 620)

Tierney, W. G., and Rhoads, R. A. (1993). *Enhancing promotion, tenure and beyond: Faculty socialization as a cultural process.* ASHE-ERIC Higher Education Report, no. 6.

Washington, DC: Association for the Study of Higher Education. (ED 368 322)

Tobias, S. (1992). *Revitalizing undergraduate science: Why some things work and most don't.* Tucson, AZ: Research Corporation. (ED 357 975)

Tobias, S. (1995, January 19). *Department-based audit of undergraduate instruction.* Paper presented at the American Association for Higher Education Forum on Faculty Roles and Rewards, Phoenix, AZ.

Toombs, W., and Escala, M. J. (1987). *Doing the right thing: Problems of academic organization.* Paper presented at the Annual Meeting of the Association for the Study of Higher Education, February 13–17, San Diego, CA. (ED 281 441)

Toombs, W., and Tierney, W. G. (1991). *Meeting the mandate: Renewing the college and department curriculum.* ASHE-ERIC Higher Education Report, no. 6. Washington, DC: George Washington University, Graduate School of Education and Human Development. (ED 345 603)

Traub, J. (1997, October 20 and 27). Drive-thru U. *New Yorker,* 114–122.

Tucker, A. (1993). *Chairing the academic department* (3rd ed.). Washington, DC: American Council on Education/Oryx.

University of California at Los Angeles Higher Education Research Institute. (1997). *The American college teacher: National norms for the 1995–96 HERI faculty survey.* Los Angeles: Author.

Volkwein, J. F., and Carbone, D. A. (1994). The impact of departmental research and teaching climates on undergraduate growth and satisfaction. *Journal of Higher Education, 65*(2), 147–167.

Walvoord, B. E., Hunt, L. L., Dowling, E. F., and McMahon, J. (1997). *In the long run: A study of faculty in three writing-across-the-curriculum programs.* Urbana, IL: National Council of Teachers of English. (ED 402 589)

Webster, D. S., and Skinner, T. (1996, May/June). Rating Ph.D. programs: What the NRC report says . . . and doesn't say. *Change, 28*(3), 22–44.

Weick, K. E. (1983). Contradictions in a community of scholars: The cohesion-accuracy tradeoff. *Review of Higher Education, 6*(4), 253–267.

Weimer, M. (1993, November/December). The disciplinary journals on pedagogy. *Change, 25*(6), 44–51.

Wergin, J. F. (1994). *The collaborative department: How five campuses are inching toward cultures of collective responsibility.* Washington, DC: American Association for Higher Education. (ED 406 958)

Wergin, J. F. (1999, December). Evaluating department achievements: Consequences for the work of faculty. *AAHE Bulletin, 52*(4), 3–6.

Whalen, E. L. (1991). *Responsibility center budgeting: An approach to decentralized management for institutions of higher education.* Bloomington, IN: Indiana University Press. (ED 340 301)

White, T. H. (1990). Constructive linking: Toward a matrix approach in higher education. In M. E. Clark and S. A. Wawrytko (Eds.), *Rethinking the curriculum: Toward an integrated, interdisciplinary college education* (pp. 107–120). New York: Greenwood Press.

Wilger, A. K., and Massy, W. F. (1993, November). Prospects for restructuring: A sampling of the faculty climate. *Pew Policy Perspectives, 5*(2), Section B.

Willcoxson, L., and Walker, P. (1995). Valuing teaching: A strategy for changing the organisational culture of an academic department. *Higher Education Research and Development, 14*(2), 269–278.

Williams, L. P. (1956). Democracy and hierarchy: A profile of faculty meetings in department "X." *Journal of Educational Sociology, 30,* 168–172.

Winston, G. C. (1999, January/February). For-profit higher education: Godzilla or Chicken Little? *Change, 31*(1), 12–19.

Wright, W. A. (1994, Summer). Heads hold key to faculty development. *Department Chair, 2–3.*

Young, J. R. (1999, May 7). A virtual student teaches himself. *Chronicle of Higher Education, A31.*

Zemsky, R. (1991, November). Learning slope. *Policy Perspectives, 4,* 1A–8A.

Zemsky, R. (1993, May/June). On reversing the ratchet: Restructuring in colleges and universities. *Change, 25,* 56–62.

Zemsky, R. (1995a, January 20). *The department as a fulcrum for change.* Presentation at the American Association for Higher Education Third Conference on Faculty Roles and Rewards, Phoenix, AZ. (Audiotape)

Zemsky, R. (1995b, June 12). *The department as a fulcrum for change.* Presentation at the American Association for Higher Education Conference on Assessment and Quality, Boston, MA. (Audiotape)

Zemsky, R. (1996, February). Double agent. *Policy Perspectives*. Pew Higher Education Roundtable. (ED 394 366)

Zemsky, R. (Ed.). (1991, November). *Policy Perspectives*. Pew Higher Education Research Project.

Zemsky, R., and Massy, W. F. (1995, November/December). Toward understanding of our current predicaments: Expanding perimeters, melting cores, and sticky functions. *Change, 27*(6), 40–49.

NAME INDEX

A

Adam, B. E., 28, 80
Adams, E. H., 1–2
Ahmed, E., 51, 87
Alexander, L. T., 36
Alpert, D., 25, 89
Anderson, C., 9, 14, 17, 48
Anderson, G. L., 48
Anderson, M. S., 17
Angelo, T. A., 3, 6, 7, 87, 95
Ardizzone, T., 77
Argyris, C., 6, 17, 89
Armajani, B., 25
Armstrong, L., Jr., 72
Aronowitz, S., 49
Astin, A. W., 10, 27, 36
Austin, A. E., 3, 26, 57, 89

B

Bailey, J., 19, 88–89
Baldridge, J. V., 15, 25, 34, 42
Banta, T. W., 1–2, 14, 72
Bare, A. C., 19, 35, 70, 88–89
Barr, R. B., 10
Bassis, M., 62
Bates, A. W., 10
Becher, T., 2, 3, 16, 25, 34, 39
Benjamin, R., 42
Bennett, J. B., 58
Bensimon, E. M., 3, 57, 59, 60, 62–63, 78
Bergquist, W. H., 16, 18, 19, 20, 42, 47, 60, 70
Berlin, W., 51, 87–88
Bess, J. L., 29
Biglan, A., 26
Billingsley, J. M., 37
Birnbaum, R., 3, 37, 42, 47, 53–54, 70
Black, K. E., 1–2, 14, 72
Blackburn, R. T., 66
Blandy, R., 36
Blomquist, D., 77
Boice, R., 75, 81
Bolman, L. G., 3, 49
Bolton, C. K., 19, 88–89
Bowen, H., 50, 70
Boyer, E. L., 25, 66, 80–81
Boyer, R. K., 19, 88–89
Braxton, J. M., 26–27

Bresser, R. K., 26
Brown, J. S., 6
Brown, W. R., 42, 43, 53, 66, 77
Brunton, B., 51, 87
Burke, D. L., 27

C

Cambridge, B. L., 14
Cameron, K. S., 19, 20
Cannon, R. A., 36, 87
Carbone, D. A., 1
Carey, A. K., 8
Carroll, J. B., 26–27, 58
Carroll, S., 42
Chaffee, E. E., 20
Clark, B. R., 6, 7, 25, 27, 31, 36, 42, 43, 54
Clark, M. E., 25
Colbeck, C., 6
Colton, J., 40, 51–52
Conrad, C. F., 36, 42
Constanza, R., 25
Content, R., 27
Creswell, J. W., 58, 59, 62–63
Crockett, C., 19, 88–89
Crothers, C., 48, 49, 76
Cureton, J. S., 10
Curtis, D. V., 15, 25, 34, 42

D

Dahlgren, L. O., 26
David, P., 31, 42
Davis, R. H., 36
Dawkins, P., 36
Deal, T. E., 3, 49
Deetz, S. A., 57, 59, 60
Diamond, R. M., 13, 28, 36, 80
Dill, D. D., 16, 25, 50, 57, 58, 61, 63, 87
Dill, W. R., 9
Dodge, L. D., 66
Dowling, E. F., 78
Durst, R., 79
Dworkin, T., 77

E

Easterby-Smith, M., 21, 36
Ecker, G. P., 15, 25, 34, 42
Edington, D. W., 66

Edwards, R., 2, 16, 57, 59, 60, 61
Elton, C. F., 26
Epstein, L. D., 16, 34, 39
Escala, M. J., 3, 25, 49
Ettington, D. R., 19, 20
Ewell, P. T., 3, 4, 11, 29

F
Fairweather, J., 80, 81
Falk, G., 59
Filan, G. L., 63
Fink, L. D., 74
Finnegan, D. E., 28, 87–88
Fleming, W., 6
Foote, E., 63
Forman, S., 19, 88–89
Francis, J. G., 54
Frantz, C. M., 9
Froh, R. C., 76
Fulmer, K. A., 36
Fulton, R. D., 70, 75

G
Gamson, Z. F., 28, 87–88
Gannicott, K., 36
Gappa, J. M., 70, 75
Gardiner, L. F., 1–2, 13–14
Gidley, J., 1
Gilbert, S. W., 10
Gillett-Karam, R., 62–63
Gilley, J. W., 36
Gilliland, M. W., 87
Gmelch, W. H., 3, 20, 26–27, 58, 62–63, 77
Goethals, G. R., 9
Green, K. C., 10
Green, M. F., 9
Groner, N. E., 26–27, 36, 48
Guskin, A. E., 11, 62, 71
Guskin, S., 77

H
Hackman, J. D., 39
Hampton, M. C., 54
Hansen, 41
Hardy, C., 41
Hargens, L. L., 26–27
Haworth, J. G., 36, 42

Hayward, P. C., 26–27
Hearn, J. C., 76
Hecht, I., 62–63
Heller, J. F., 6, 19, 89
Hemphill, J. K., 61
Heterick, R. C., Jr., 10
Hewton, E., 19, 88–89
Heydinger, R. B., 25
Higgerson, M. L., 62–63
Hinni, J. B., 3, 43
Hirst, L., 77
Hobbs, W. C., 48
Holden, M. C., 61
Holland, J. L, 27
Horowitz, S. M., 66
Huber, B. J., 26–27
Hunt, L. L., 78
Hussain, M. N., 36
Hutchinson, P, 25

I

Inayatullah, S., 1

J

Janzow, F. T., 3, 43
Jermier, J. M., 59
Johnson, J. R., 3, 43
Jordan, J. M., 26–27

K

Kahn, S., 39–40
Kain, P., 36
Karseth, B., 17
Kasper, W., 36
Katz, M. B., 43
Keller, G., 42–43
Kennedy, D., 1, 15
Kerr, S., 59
Klein, T., 1
Klos, D., 66
Knight, W. H., 61
Kogan, M., 2, 3, 16, 25, 34, 39
Kohen, A. I., 51, 87
Kozma, R. B., 57
Kressel, K., 19, 88–89
Kriegler, R., 36
Kuh, G. D., 15, 19

L

Lamber, J., 77
Lame, J-E., n
Lane, J-E., 15
Langley, A., 41
Larson, R. S., 3, 57, 58, 78
Lattuca, L. R., 25, 26
Layzell, D. T., 1, 80
Lazerson, M., 72
Leslie, D. W., 59, 75
Levin, H. M., 35, 38
Levine, A., 10, 31, 43
Licata, C., 81
Lincoln, Y. S., 33, 35
Loftis, J. E., 51–52
Lonsdale, A. J., 36, 87
Louis, K. S., 17
Lovrich, N. P., 77
Lucas, A. F., 3, 58, 59, 60, 62–63, 82, 87–88
Lucero, C., 65
Lueddeke, G. R., 57, 61
Lund, J. P., 1–2, 14, 72

M

Machung, A., 28
Manns, C. L., 66
March, J. G., 66
Marchese, T., 9, 10
Massy, W. F., 6, 7, 31, 39, 40, 42, 47, 53, 66, 70, 71
Mathias, H., 6
McAdams, R. P., 61
McCarthy, M., 61
McCormack, P., 19
McKeachie, W. J., 60
McMahon, J., 78
Meador, M., 26–27
Menges, R. J., 76
Mets, L. A., 1–2
Michael, S. O., 9
Middaugh, M., 38
Miller, M. T., 58
Milliman, S., 51, 87
Mingle, J. R., 10
Mintzberg, H., 41
Miskin, V. D., 3, 62–63
Mitchell, M. B., 57, 61
Mohrman, K., 52, 53, 66
Moxley, J. M., 59

S

Salancik, G. R., 34–35, 39
Sanders, K., 62–63
Schein, E. H., 12, 17, 19, 21, 22, 88–89
Schmidt, P., 9
Schoenfeld, C., 18
Scholten, I., 19
Schön, D. A., 6, 17, 89
Schultz, L., 79
Schuster, J., 50, 65, 70
Seagren, A. T., 58, 59, 62–63
Senge, P. M., 3, 6, 57, 63, 89
Seymour, D. T., 2, 37–38
Sherr, L. A., 20
Shumanis, N., 72
Simpson, D. J., 49
Simpson, W. A., 38
Skinner, T., 25
Smart, J. C., 19, 26, 47, 50, 53, 53–54, 70, 87
Smelser, N. J., 27
Smith, B., 19, 51, 54, 88–89
Smith, H. L., 77, 81
Smith, P., 9, 78
Smith, V. R., 51, 87
Soled, S., 8
Sorcinelli, M. D., 74
Sperber, W. E., 38
St. John, E. P., 19, 47, 50, 53, 53–54, 70, 87
Stark, J. S., 25, 26
Stevens, D., 51, 87
Stoecker, J. L., 26
Strand, R., 36
Sykes, C. J., 9

T

Tagg, J., 10
Terenzini, P. T., 1
Thelen, D., 77
Theus, K. T., 37
Thomas, C., 49
Tierney, W. G., 3, 18, 19, 42–43, 71, 74, 75
Tobias, S., 14, 51, 87–88
Toombs, W., 3, 25, 49
Traub, J., 29
Tucker, A., 52, 62–63
Twigg, C. A., 10

V

Van Horn-Grassmeyer, K., 58
Volkwein, J. F., 1

W

Wagener, U., 72
Walker, C. J., 76
Walker, P., 1
Walters, S.J.K., 26–27
Walvoord, B. E., 8, 12, 30, 43–44, 73, 77, 78, 81
Ward, K., 62–63
Wawrytko, S. A., 25
Webster, D. S., 25
Weick, K. E., 17
Weimer, M., 30
Wergin, J. F., 6, 7, 20, 38, 53, 54, 78
Whalen, E. L., 1–2
Wheeler, D. W., 58, 59, 62–63
White, T. H., 18, 43
Whitt, E. J., 15, 19
Wilger, A. K., 6
Wilke, P. K., 77
Willcoxson, L., 1
Williams, L. P., 48
Winston, G. C., 9

Y

Young, J. R., 70

Z

Zemsky, R., 1, 2, 9, 31, 39, 42, 57, 71, 73

SUBJECT INDEX

A

Academic belief system, 10–11
Academic freedom, 16
Adhocracy, 86–87
Administrative roles (case history), 43–46
Allegiances, multiple, 58–59
Alternative structures, 42
American Association for Higher Education, 14, 39; Faculty Roles and Rewards Conference, 39
Assessment Update, 14
Authority. *See* Power
Autonomy, departmental: building of, 36; sources of, 33–35; and top-down change, 35; as value, 16

B

Bush Foundation, 78

C

Carnegie Foundation for Advancement of Teaching, 29, 31
Carnegie Project for the Scholarship of Teaching and Learning, 28, 81
Cell model, 22
Central administration: departmental relations with, 33–46; relationship of department to, 92–93; role of, in facilitating departmental change, 35–43
Central Pennsylvania Consortium, 78
Change, 40
Change, departmental: and academic belief system, 11–12; and assessing outcomes, 13–14; four-step process for, 3–7, 86; local agenda for, 85–87; national agenda for, 88–89; need for, 1–2; political and economic pressures for, 9; potential for, 2; and reading departmental environment, 12–13; research agenda for, 87–88; and student expectations and attitudes, 10; and student population, 10; and student reasons for attending school, 10; and technological advances, 10
Chronicle of Higher Education, The, 12
Clan culture, 47–48, 50
Collaboration, 36–37
Collegial organizations: and difficulty evaluating outcomes and assigning differential rewards based on outcomes, 52–53; exploitation in, 49; implications for change in, 50–54; importance of respect in, 48–49; inward *versus* outward orientation of, 53; time and consensus limitations of, 51–52
Collegiality: authentic, 6–7; and collegial guidance, 74–75; culture of, 18–19; and increase in collegial interaction, 78
Competition, 77
Consensus, 51–52
Context, chair leadership dependence on, 57–58

Core and cloud model, 30

Crises, management of, 41

Culture: broad understanding of, 3; and coexisting cultures, 18–19; departmental, 18–19; influence of, in faculty rewards, 75; leadership analysis of, 60; and managerial, 18–19; and negotiating culture, 18–19

D

Deadlines, management of, 41

Decision making. *See* Organization, departmental

Disciplines: and alternative structures, 30–31; and changing disciplinary society, 28; characteristics of, and avenues for change, 91–92; collaboration among, 30; and departments, 25–31; differences among, 26–27, 28; and focus on specialization, 73–74; and hiring pool, 29–30; influence of, on departments, 27–28; and interdisciplinarity, 25–26

Duke University, 70

E

Educause, 12

Engineering Education, 30

Entrepreneurialism, 86–87

Environment, assessment of, 12–13

Evaluation, 52–53

Expertise, 16

Exxon Foundation, 57

F

Faculty: ambiguous performance standards for, 77; change in attitudes, values, skills of, 78; and collegial guidance, 74–75; departmental rewards for, 75–76; differential control over hiring of, 72–73; and focus on disciplinary specialization, 73–74; and formal orientation, 74; socialization and development of, 74–75

Fairleigh Dickinson University, 82

Fiscal incentives, 39–41

Flexibility, 11, 80

Framing, 13; for viewing departmental organization, 47–49

Fund for the Improvement of Post-Secondary Education, 28

G

Gatekeeping, 28

Goals, definition of, 13

Great Lakes College Association, 78

H

Higher Education Research Institute (University of California at Los Angeles), 48–49, 50

Hiring, 27, 29–30, 72–73, 79–80

I

Ideal department, vision of, 6–7, 95
Indiana University, 70
Indianapolis Assess Conference, 14
Information, gathering and interpretation of, 37–39
Institute for Research in Higher Education, 9
Institutional subcultures, 18–19
Interaction. *See* Organization, departmental
Interdisciplinarity, 25–26; and collaboration, 30; and interdiscipli-
    nary knowledge, 11. *See also* Disciplines
International Alliance of Teacher Scholars, 30

J

Journal of Teaching Excellence, 30
Journals, 30

K

Kansas Regents universities, 41

L

Leadership, departmental: ambiguous power in, 59–60; dependence
    of, on context, 57–58; development of, 62–63; formal training for,
    60; hero style of, 62; mediator style of, 62; and multiple alle-
    giances and tasks, 58–59; summary of characteristics of, and
    avenues of change, 93–94; team style of, 62; working with, 41
Learning department: building, 12–13, 19, 31, 82; guidelines for
    achieving, 7; and learning paradigm, 10–11
Lehigh University, 61
Lilly Endowment, 28, 78

M

Managerial culture, 18–19
Mentoring, 17
Michigan State University, 36
Mission, 13
Mission, shared, 36–37

N

National Association of Biology Teachers, 30
National Center for Educational Statistics, 9, 10
National Science Foundation, 57
National Survey of Student Engagement (NSSE), 29
Negotiating culture, 18–19
NSSE. *See* National Survey of Student Engagement

O

Oligarchic organization, 47–49
Ontario, 43

Organization, departmental: and collegial departments, 47; exploring new models for, 53–54; mixed models in, 49; multiple frames for viewing, 47–49; and oligarchic, feudal, or caste-based, 47–49; summary of characteristics of, and avenues of change, 93

Orientation: formal, 74; inward *versus* outward, 53

Outcomes, assessment of, 11, 13–14, 72

P

Performance standards, 77

Pew Charitable Trusts, 28, 30

Pew Forum on Undergraduate Learning, 29

Pew Higher Education Roundtable, 12, 47, 57

Pew Preparing Future Faculty Project, 30

PIRT. *See* Project to Improve and Reward Teaching

Power: ambiguous, of department chair, 59–60; change in, of chair, 91; departmental sources of, 33–35

Project to Improve and Reward Teaching (PIRT), 8, 38, 41, 43–45, 47, 51

Public Agenda, 9

Q

Quality control, 78–79

R

Rankings, criteria for, 29

RCM. *See* Responsibility-centered management

Reason, 17

Responsibility-centered management (RCM), 40

Review, criteria for, 29

Rewards, faculty: change in system of, 81; and effects of competition on collegial traditions, 77; and influence of culture, 75; intrinsic and extrinsic, 76

S

Scholarship, 28, 80–81

Scientific method, 17

Service, 17

Socialization, 27–28, 74–75

Southeast Missouri State University, 43

Specialization, 16, 19, 73–74

State University of New York at Buffalo, 31, 43

Strategy: definition of, 13; six categories of, 4–6; and strategic planning, 60–61

Students: expectations and attitudes of, 10; and makeup of student population, 10; reasons of, for attending school, 10

Subcultures, institutional, 18–19, 22

Syracuse University, 28, 80

T

Tasks, multiple, 58–59
Teaching paradigm, *versus* learning paradigm, 10–11
Team concept, 20
Technology, advances in, 10
TLT Group, 12
Total Quality Management, 20
Training, for department chairs, 60
Trust, 36–37

U

University governance, forums for, 42–43
University of California at Los Angeles, 48–49, 50
University of Cincinnati, 8, 39, 41, 43, 45, 47, 61, 77, 79, 88
University of Indiana, 40
University of Southern California, 40

V

Values, academic: and academic freedom, 16; and autonomy, 16;
building on, 20; and change, 20–21; coexisting cultures and,
18–19; and collegiality, 15–16; espoused *versus* actual, 17–18;
examination of departmental, 19; five core, 15–17; and reason
and scientific method, 17; redefinition of, 21–22; and service and
mentoring, 17; and specialization/expertise, 16; summary of
characteristics of, 17–18

W

Western Governor's University, 70
Whitworth College (Spokane, Washington), 30
Work, departmental: and allocation of tasks, 70; and assessment of
outcomes, 72; changes in, 67–69; collective responsibility for, 78;
and enhancement of productivity, 71; multiple influences on
definition of, 65–66; quality control of, 71–72; redefinition of,
through disciplinary associations, 80–81; summary of characteristics of, and avenues of change, 94
World Wide Web, 1

ASHE-ERIC HIGHER EDUCATION REPORTS

The mission of the Educational Resources Information Center (ERIC) system is to improve American education by increasing and facilitating the use of educational research and information on practice in the activities of learning, teaching, educational decision making, and research, wherever and whenever these activities take place.

Since 1983, the ASHE-ERIC Higher Education Report series has been published in cooperation with the Association for the Study of Higher Education (ASHE). Starting in 2000, the series is published by Jossey-Bass in conjunction with the ERIC Clearinghouse on Higher Education.

Each monograph is the definitive analysis of a tough higher education problem, based on thorough research of pertinent literature and institutional experiences. Topics are identified by a national survey. Noted practitioners and scholars are then commissioned to write the reports, with experts providing critical reviews of each manuscript before publication.

Eight monographs (10 before 1985) in the ASHE-ERIC Higher Education Report series are published each year and are available on individual and subscription bases. To order, use the order form at the back of this volume.

Qualified persons interested in writing a monograph for the ASHE-ERIC Higher Education Report series are invited to submit a proposal to the National Advisory Board. As the preeminent literature review and issue analysis series in higher education, the Higher Education Reports are guaranteed wide dissemination and provide national exposure for accepted candidates. Execution of a monograph requires at least a minimal familiarity with the ERIC database, including *Resources in Education* and the current *Index to Journals in Education*. The objective of these reports is to bridge conventional wisdom and practical research.

ADVISORY BOARD

CONSULTING EDITORS AND
REVIEW PANELISTS

Marilyn J. Amey
University of Kansas

Sally Atkins
Appalachian State University

John M. Braxton
Vanderbilt University

A. Leigh DeNeef
Duke University

Kassie Freeman
Vanderbilt University

Linda K. Johnsrud
University of Hawaii

Elizabeth A. Jones
Pennsylvania State University

Susan Kahn
Indiana University–Purdue University Indianapolis

William Plater
Indiana University–Purdue University Indianapolis

Robert Secor
Pennsylvania State University

Carolyn Thompson
SUNY–Buffalo

Jon Wergin
Virginia Commonwealth University

Elizabeth J. Whitt
University of Illinois–Chicago

Volume 27 ASHE-ERIC Higher Education Reports

1. The Art and Science of Classroom Assessment: The Missing Part of Pedagogy
   Susan M. Brookhart

2. Due Process and Higher Education: A Systemic Approach to Fair Decision Making
   Ed Stevens

3. Grading Students' Classroom Writing: Issues and Strategies
   Bruce W. Speck

4. Posttenure Faculty Development: Building a System for Faculty Improvement and Appreciation
   Jeffrey W. Alstete

5. Digital Dilemma: Issues of Access, Cost, and Quality in Media-Enhanced and Distance Education
   Gerald C. Van Dusen

6. Women and Minority Faculty in the Academic Workplace: Recruitment, Retention, and Academic Culture
   Adalberto Aguirre, Jr.

7. Higher Education Outside of the Academy
   Jeffrey A. Cantor

Volume 26 ASHE-ERIC Higher Education Reports

1. Faculty Workload Studies: Perspectives, Needs, and Future Directions
   Katrina A. Meyer

2. Assessing Faculty Publication Productivity: Issues of Equity
   Elizabeth G. Creamer

3. Proclaiming and Sustaining Excellence: Assessment as a Faculty Role
   Karen Maitland Schilling and Karl L. Schilling

4. Creating Learning Centered Classrooms: What Does Learning Theory Have to Say?
   Frances K. Stage, Patricia A. Muller, Jillian Kinzie, and Ada Simmons

5. The Academic Administrator and the Law: What Every Dean and Department Chair Needs to Know
   J. Douglas Toma and Richard L. Palm

6. The Powerful Potential of Learning Communities: Improving Education for the Future
   Oscar T. Lenning and Larry H. Ebbers

7. Enrollment Management for the 21st Century: Institutional Goals, Accountability, and Fiscal Responsibility
   Garlene Penn

8. Enacting Diverse Learning Environments: Improving the Climate for Racial/Ethnic Diversity in Higher Education
   Sylvia Hurtado, Jeffrey Milem, Alma Clayton-Pedersen, and Walter Allen

Volume 25 ASHE-ERIC Higher Education Reports

1. A Culture for Academic Excellence: Implementing the Quality Principles in Higher Education
   Jann E. Freed, Marie R. Klugman, and Jonathan D. Fife

2. From Discipline to Development: Rethinking Student Conduct in Higher Education
   Michael Dannells

3. Academic Controversy: Enriching College Instruction Through Intellectual Conflict
   David W. Johnson, Roger T. Johnson, and Karl A. Smith

4. Higher Education Leadership: Analyzing the Gender Gap
   Luba Chliwniak

5. The Virtual Campus: Technology and Reform in Higher Education
   Gerald C. Van Dusen

6. Early Intervention Programs: Opening the Door to Higher Education
   Robert H. Fenske, Christine A. Geranios, Jonathan E. Keller, and David E. Moore

7. The Vitality of Senior Faculty Members: Snow on the Roof— Fire in the Furnace
   Carole J. Bland and William H. Bergquist

8. A National Review of Scholastic Achievement in General Education: How Are We Doing and Why Should We Care?
   Steven J. Osterlind

Volume 24 ASHE-ERIC Higher Education Reports

1. Tenure, Promotion, and Reappointment: Legal and Administrative Implications
   Benjamin Baez and John A. Centra

2. Taking Teaching Seriously: Meeting the Challenge of Instructional Improvement
   Michael B. Paulsen and Kenneth A. Feldman

3. Empowering the Faculty: Mentoring Redirected and Renewed
   Gaye Luna and Deborah L. Cullen

4. Enhancing Student Learning: Intellectual, Social, and Emotional Integration
   Anne Goodsell Love and Patrick G. Love

5. Benchmarking in Higher Education: Adapting Best Practices to Improve Quality
   Jeffrey W. Alstete

Back Issue/Subscription Order Form

Copy or detach and send to:
Jossey-Bass, 350 Sansome Street, San Francisco CA 94104-1342

Call or fax toll free!
Phone 888-378-2537 6AM-5PM PST; Fax 800-605-2665

Individual reports:

Please send me the following reports at $24 each
(Important: please include series initials and issue number, such as AEHE 27:1)

1. AEHE _____

_____

_____

$ _____ Total for individual reports

$ _____ Shipping charges (for individual reports *only;* subscriptions are exempt from shipping charges): Up to $30, add $5^{50} • $30^{01}–$50, add $6^{50} $50^{01}–$75, add $8 • $75^{01}–$100, add $10 • $100^{01}–$150, add $12 Over $150, call for shipping charge

Subscriptions

Please ❑ start ❑ renew my subscription to *ASHE-ERIC Higher Education Reports* for the year <u>2000</u> at the following rate (8 issues):   U.S.: $144   Canada: $169   All others: $174

Please ❑ start my subscription to *ASHE-ERIC Higher Education Reports* for the year <u>2001</u> at the following rate (6 issues): U.S.: $108   Canada: $188   All others: $256

NOTE: Subscriptions are for the calendar year only. Subscriptions begin with Report 1 of the year indicated above.

$ _____ Total individual reports and subscriptions (Add appropriate sales tax for your state for individual reports. No sales tax on U.S. subscriptions. Canadian residents, add GST for subscriptions and individual reports.)

❑ Payment enclosed (U.S. check or money order only)

❑ VISA, MC, AmEx, Discover Card # _____ Exp. date _____

Signature _____ Day phone _____

❑ Bill me (U.S. institutional orders only. Purchase order required.)

Purchase order #_____

Federal Tax ID 135593032   GST 89102-8052

Name _____

Address _____

_____

Phone_____ E-mail _____

For more information about Jossey-Bass, visit our Web site at:
www.josseybass.com   **PRIORITY CODE = ND1**

BARBARA E. WALVOORD directs the Kaneb Center for Teaching and Learning at the University of Notre Dame, where she is also a concurrent professor of English and a fellow of the Institute for Educational Initiatives. She was named 1987 Maryland English Teacher of the Year for Higher Education and received Notre Dame's presidential award in 1999.

ANNA K. CAREY is professor emerita of English at the University of Cincinnati Clermont College, where she served as division chair, director of freshman English competency testing, and chair of general education. She was a founder and cochair of the Project to Improve and Reward Teaching.

HOKE L. SMITH is president of Towson University in Maryland, where he has sponsored and participated in a highly successful faculty, chair, and staff leadership development program. He has been chair of the American Association of State Colleges and Universities and of the American Council on Education.

SUZANNE W. SOLED is associate professor of educational foundation at the University of Cincinnati. She has served as director of programs for honors students, developmental studies, and faculty development, including the Project to Improve and Reward Teaching.

PHILIP K. WAY is director of the University Honors Scholars Program at the University of Cincinnati, where he is associate professor and was formerly assistant head and director of undergraduate studies in economics. Recipient of two National Science Foundation grants to enhance the teaching of economics, he also has codirected the Project to Improve and Reward Teaching.

DEBBIE ZORN is director of the University of Cincinnati Evaluation Services Center, which assists more than 40 universities, schools, and social services agencies with assessment and evaluation. She has been an instructional specialist and program coordinator at the University of Cincinnati, as well as an adjunct instructor in educational foundations and a secondary school English teacher.